The Vanished Landmarks Game

Published by Blue Cat Bistro

First Edition, First Printing

All of the material in this collection was originally published elsewhere. The Bunkhouse appeared in *The Berkshire Review* and as a *Rutland Herald* People and Places feature. Other past People and Places features include: The Vermonter Who Came Home, Fair Haven Boy, and Visiting My Father at the Old Soldiers' Home. All other material was first published in the *Rutland Herald Express*.

ISBN 978-0-615-73010-3

Design: Toelke Associates, Chatham, NY   www.toelkeassociates.com

Cover photo by Wenger Rehlen: Old maples lining Frisbee Hill Road in Castleton, Vermont.

The Vanished Landmarks Game

Vermont Stories from West of Birdseye

Pamela Hayes Rehlen

Blue Cat Bistro • Castleton, Vermont

This is for my husband
who's made everything possible.

Contents

Introduction

Three years ago, Randal Smathers, at that time the managing editor of the *Rutland Herald,* called up and asked if he could come out to Castleton and talk to me.

Over a period of years I'd written a number of articles for the *Herald*. I wrote a Sunday Magazine cover story on the reborn local slate industry—at that time booming— and I wrote another Sunday Magazine cover story, illustrated by cartoonist Jeff Danziger, on *The Truly Terrible Houseguest.*

But what suited me best was writing 2,000 word pieces for the *People and Places* section of the paper. However, I didn't very often turn out these pieces and submit them unsolicited, *'throw them over the transom,'* in the slang of the trade.

When Randal and I met for lunch at the Birdseye Diner, he said he had a writing proposition. Would I do a weekly column for a paper he was putting together called the *Rutland Herald Express* aimed at covering life in the towns surrounding Rutland? Of course I said I'd consider it, but I didn't think I would be able to turn out a column every week. That was a daunting proposition. We had a nice chat, and I went home and thought about it awhile.

I wrote up a piece on the little Jimmy Lynch farmhouse in the center of campus that Castleton State College was in the process of tearing down because the school had decided it wanted to build a parking lot on the land.

I sent that in. It became the first of my, what are now approximately 170, weekly columns.

It seems to me to be Fate—in which I believe strongly—that brought Randal out to Castleton with his proposal.

He gave me an opportunity to do something that I never would have taken on by myself. The continual deadlines have pushed me to make calls and make visits and think about my surroundings, the people and the places and the old stories.

Harry O'Rourke, an Old Irish, born in Castleton January 1, 1900, a logger and farmer, but most of all a horseman. the last to continue to go into the woods with a team. (O'Rourke family collection)

I tell my husband that sometimes I feel I'm sitting in front of a vast puzzle, the kind that gets put out on a table and worked on for months.

Every interview I do with people who have been in Castleton, or Hubbardton, or Hydeville, for generations allows me to push another puzzle piece into place. The design of the whole grows clearer.

I value connection above all things – connection to land and connection to people—and as the puzzle takes shape, I see how connected everyone and everything around here is.

Castleton is a community and a culture built on farms and farming. Castletonians were still buying into lives of agriculture as late as the 1960s.

They did it because their parents had done it, and it had provided at least a marginal existence. They had farming in their blood, but by the 1960s, working the land was no longer a viable way of life.

Castleton is also a community shaped by earlier generations' pattern of having a lot of children. All the old-time Castletonians I talk to, now in their seventies or eighties, even some in their sixties, were born into very large families.

I think of Ed and Nancy Doran, friends of and contemporaries of my parents, who had eleven or twelve children. Brian Traverse, now in his fifties, was one of twelve. Frannie Bruno Gray told me about her family of ten. Ray Ladd was one of eight.

Most of these children whom economic factors pushed off the land didn't move away. They stayed around. They built little modern houses and settled near their parents.

They found jobs at Rutland's General Electric plant. They went to work for the post office. Some became carpenters. Some started their own businesses: septic services, trash removal, lawn maintenance, slate roofing. The many Doran sons who went into successful service-oriented enterprises are an example of this.

I always say that it's unwise to find fault with anyone because whomever you're sharing your censoriousness insight with is probably a first or second cousin.

Castleton is a community of clans. Some old-time local people are Yankees, some Italian, some French, but what most of them are is Irish. There are the minority Protestant Irish and the majority Catholic Irish. The Catholic Irish seem to me to be a more colorful lot.

My father always spoke—often resignedly—about Fair Haven's *Old Irish,* by that he meant a group of people who exhibited an unmistakable, sometimes perverse, way of looking at things.

Harry O'Rourke's November 1987 funeral procession from Castleton's Saint John's Catholic Church to the Hillside Cemetery. (O'Rourke family collection)

But I've come to admire the Celtic world view. Perhaps it was their loyalty, occasional self-destructiveness, and general perversity that kept the Irish on the land around Castleton the longest. Sometimes that stubbornness paid off. The O'Rourkes with their equine empire come to mind.

I will never forget patriarch Harry O'Rourke's years-ago funeral with a line of horse-draw carriages heading down Main Street to St. John's Church.

Only the Catholic Irish would have thought of, and carried out, that funeral.

▲▲▲

I grew up hearing stories. My parents knew everyone in Castleton—and for that matter everyone in Fair Haven. Which didn't make them unique; there was a time around here when everyone knew everyone.

This was a small, closed, world. People also knew other peoples' families, mothers and fathers, and they had a good grasp of other peoples' foibles, their strengths and weaknesses. The culture was still shaped by survival skills and instincts. Political correctness was an unimaginable attitude.

Fools weren't tolerated, unless their foolishness had a humorous aspect, and in that case they were cherished as an endless source of good material. The best raconteurs were prized, and two of the very best, to my mind, were Martha Towers and Margaret Onion.

Even as a young person, I would laugh until I wept when Martha, abetted by her husband Bucky, got going. The best stories were remembered and repeated and handed down.

I tried to do that myself by recounting the "Eat it Cassius" story in my Fair Haven Boy essay. And I tried to give an idea of Martha, now a hundred years old, in my Martha Towers column.

Margaret Onion was a more refined individual, originally from Dorset. She had gone to Smith College and come back to marry a town father and teach English literature at Fair Haven High School.

She was as funny, as sharp and insightful, as Martha. I remember one Sunday morning standing after church in front of the Federated with Martha and Margaret and Hulda Cole, Margaret telling stories about old characters in Dorset, and it was so wonderful I thought, 'I will never hear anything as funny as this as long as I live.'

And I haven't.

I think people became good story tellers because they had to amuse themselves, and they recognized wonderful material right at hand. I interviewed Fran Gray, now in her early eighties, for a Castleton's South Street three-part column, and that's what she thought too.

Now, I tell stories. I love the cultural history and the connections. It comes naturally, and I'm reflecting what I've heard and experienced. What gives me the greatest joy is to see my son telling stories, to see him also delighting in the experiences of his Castleton life.

A lot of the material in this book is about my family, about the Gibbses, my mother's people, and about my Hayes father and his mother. I tend to forget that my mother was interested in people too, and like my father talked about them told stories about them.

What both my parents gave me was the gift of context and their own perspective. When I was younger, I tried to remember all my parents' material. I struggled not to let it get away.

But there were so many names and so many intricate connections. Who's grandfather had been the butcher in Fair Haven, or the barber? Who drank? Who ran off with someone else's wife? Who was glad to have their wife run off? What did they say, still repeated around town, when they learned that their wife had run off?

What priest had fathered a child on a visit to a back country hill farm? (endlessly retold with malicious glee by the local Protestant community.) Who absconded with a slate quarry company's weekly payroll? What was the real reason they got away with it? What kindly confirmed bachelor loved to arrange overnight camping trips with young boys?

I've lost so much of this information. It's slipped away. But lately something's come to me that I never realized earlier. Part of the reason I no can longer remember all of my parents' social, cultural world is that it's been crowded out by all I know from my own social, cultural world.

I have my own stories. I have my own connections. That's what I've written about, and collected together, in this book.

Pamela Hayes Rehlen
Castleton, Vermont
9 November 2012

The Vanished Landmarks Game

Castletonian Tommy Brough and I years ago used to play a game that came so naturally to us that for a while we didn't even realize we were playing it. Tommy worked for my husband and me at the Castleton Village Store as a meat cutter. This isn't really part of the story except to establish our long connection, but His father 'Boomer' Brough used to drive my father to Boston to the Boston University School of Education when it was in the old North End. 'Boomer' made the trip in record times it would be hard to successfully challenge today.

He loved fast cars, and his son Tommy loved horses and finally moved away to Arkansas to raise them. He's been gone a long time, but our game is something I play in my mind still.

The Vanished Landmarks Game began one day when I asked Tommy if a delivery truck went out 4A as far as Nestos. I said that without thinking. Nestos Market was a little building on the northeast corner of Drake Road and Route 4A west of Castleton Corners. In the 50s, it had been a tidy, well run grocery store, operated, as I remember, by a couple who'd come up from Connecticut. My parents liked it, and we often shopped there. As a store, it's been gone *forever.* Now it seems to be a small apartment house.

Tommy never let on that the place was long, long gone. Instead he replied, poker faced, that the delivery truck went past Nestos. It went as far out Route 4A as the Bunny Rabbit Motel.

What a grand slam answer! Almost to Hydeville, where the 'Gilbert Realty and Development' plaza, Paul's Pizza and an extensive black-topped parking area is now to be found, the Bunny Rabbit Motel was in the 50s a verdant, extensively-landscaped motel complex. It was owned by the Phillips family and advertised by a six or eight foot high wooden bunny rabbit cut-out which stood close to the road. It's impossible to imagine it now the spot is so changed.

The rules of this game were to never let on that landmarks were gone or wholly altered. It was as if there was a vanished landscape beneath the world that was presently in place, and both Tommy and I remembered and acknowledged only this earlier landscape.

Castleton's Main Street in the 1950s. (Castleton Historical Society collection)

I always liked telling Tommy something had happened out near Sherman's Beach. When I was a child it was my favorite Lake Bomoseen public swimming place. It was an old farmhouse with a sandy beach on a little peninsula at the lake's creek outlet. The old place was pulled down, a new building put up, and it became a private house with a tall cedar hedge and a garage near the road. Tommy must have swum there too.

Both he and I liked long-gone souvenir stands. Remembering how common they once were, it seems they must have been the backbone of 1950s Vermont tourist trade. I remember a place operated by two, what seemed to me then elderly women, in a stand of pines across the road from Nestos. They sold Adirondack balsam pillows, 'When you're away I pine and balsam,' and maple syrup.

There was a similar souvenir shop on old Route 4 on the north side of the road halfway to West Rutland. I almost got Tommy on that one, but then he remembered. Also, my mother's first cousin Carrie Fish had a wooden stand in front of her farmhouse just north of Castleton Corners on Route 30 with a few antiques and the usual maple syrup, maple sugar men made in St. Johnsbury, and, every August, pails of pastel gladioli.

Carrie Fish's place became the site of senior housing, the vet's clinic, a dentist's office and a lot of parking. The across-from-Nestos souvenir stand is now the site of a U-Lock-It self storage facility.

Tommy's been gone a long time, and I've never found his replacement. The Vanished Landmarks Game has to be played with a certain nostalgic attitude. It calls for looking back with a vengeance, and a take-no-prisoners disregard for change.

I miss Tommy. Just like I miss our landmarks. I particularly think of him when I say, usually to myself, 'It's out past Dunlaps barn.'

Most of my life, Dunlap's barn stood gray and dilapidated with *Dunlap* written on the side in a meadow across from my grandparents' house. It seemed impervious to years of total neglect. Then, one day, it was burned and became the site of a nursing home.

I'd say to Tommy, "It's not far. It's just past Dunlap's barn." But he isn't here, so I can't say that to him. Without him, it's become a game of solitaire.

The Manse. The author's home since 1971. (Castleton Historical Society collection)

Walking With My Mother

I read an article recently about women turning into their mothers. Researchers have found that it's inevitable, no matter how unanticipated and unwelcome, and they've pin-pointed the moment. It happens when a woman is thirty-two. I mulled this over, thinking it couldn't apply to me because I never had a very good relationship with my mother, and then I remembered, when I turned thirty-two I suddenly started to walk.

My mother was a walker. She had some inner demons with which she had to deal, and that may be the reason she covered so many miles. Growing up, I couldn't imagine anything duller. I *hated* to walk.

Every summer morning, in order to pick up the mail at the tiny Castleton post office, at that time in the west side of the Masonic Block—where Terry Riley's insurance agency is today—my mother hiked from our Pencil Mill School House, next to Boomer Brough's, down into Castleton.

*Geraldine Gibbs Hayes as a Castleton Normal School graduate and
young teacher. (Hayes family collection)*

It was a long walk, although certainly picturesque. The road was still dirt then, and my mother always greeted the old woman who sat out in front of her ramshackle house, across the road from the prosperous Eagan farm, smoking a pipe.

Occasionally my mother headed in the other direction, up the lonely Pencil Mill Road to visit her first cousin Julia Gibbs Jalbert who lived at bucolic and isolated Ledgemere Farm and took in paying summer guests. Julia owned all the land around her and had a spectacular view of Wallace Ledge which she also owned.

No one walked in those days. Walking for exercise seemed to be a foreign concept. Father of 'Burkie' Brough, mail carrier Charlie Brough, who I think was her classmate and who had taken over her father's mail route, sometimes came upon my mother swinging along a very back road. He occasionally talked her into accepting a lift, but most of the time that's the last thing she wanted.

Actually, two town ladies did walk. Hulda Saint John Cole, who lived on Main Street across from the tiny Episcopal chapel, walked a great deal, but on lady-friendly terrain. She wasn't one for heading into the hills.

And Pauline Young, the CSC school nurse, hiked into town daily from her family chicken farm out on Route 4A. Both these unusually-vigorous women looked wonderful. Hulda lived to be very old, and Pauline is still going strong.

Today, from a window in the Manse, I routinely see power walking being practiced along Main Street, but this isn't what my mother did.

I remember in the 1980s a youngish man staying at 47 Main Street, Castleton's rehabilitative half-way house, who walked every morning into Rutland to do research at the Rutland library and walked back to Castleton every night. That was impressive. Basically, he spent his life walking, and it seemed to keep him on an even keel.

I've come across local writer Ron Powers, author of the recent Ted Kennedy biography, on lonely North Poultney back roads. I recognize his kind of ruminative walking.

The author and her mother in Castleton Corners mid 1940s. (Hayes family collection)

That's the kind I do. I like to take long, long walks. Fred Michel was at one time my dentist, and I remember the spring that I had an early morning appointment with him.

Fred's office is in Poultney, and I realized that instead of driving I could try to walk. It was about eight miles, and I did it pretty easily. The only difficulties I encountered were some threatening dogs and motorists who sped alarmingly and disregarded the narrowness of the road shoulder they were sharing with me.

A natural anesthetic sets in after walking six or seven miles, so when I arrived at Fred's Church Street office I was unconcerned about any dental procedure.

Once a year, on a fine day, I walk a loop. I head up North Road out of town, then go south along the east shore of Lake Bomoseen, come down Route 30 to Castleton Corners and turn onto Route 4 heading home. This is a walk my mother would have taken in a heart beat and done far more often than once a year.

I've learned that at about seven miles, I get really tired, and then I have to just suck it up and keep going, but before that, on the right sort of day, a dreamy euphoric state of mind sets in.

When I'm walking, houses and landmarks look different. Details are clearer, and connections come to mind. A lot comes to mind.

People say to me at the store or in the diner, "I saw you out on South Street," or "I tooted at you. What were you doing yesterday walking in Fair Haven?"

All the old timers knew my mother as a walker. They always saw her on the back roads. I didn't realize it, but just like the researchers have established, at thirty-two I was fated to turn into her. My future was inescapable.

The Grands

Over its long history, Castleton has had a number of people move into town for a few years, for a decade, or for the end of a lifetime. In the nineteen fifties and in nineteen sixty, two very grand couples arrived, the Count Orlowskis and the Colonel Storms. I always think of them as *The Grands*.

They came from away. They were older and had no children and no local history. They only really mixed with people of similar pretension, and now they aren't very much remembered. But they embody a certain social era in Castleton. And one of them did a very good thing for the town.

Eric and Ethel Storm moved to Castleton when they bought a West Castleton slate house which had been a general store. Although this building must have been pretty utilitarian when it belonged to the West Castleton Slate Company, the Storms transformed it into an off-the-beaten-track country estate. They cultivated English *Country Life*-style gardens, and every once in a while they purred out of their driveway, heading to town in a Silver Cloud Rolls Royce.

The Storms were too grand for most of the locals, although I remember my Aunt Alma and Uncle Dick having them over for drinks. Drinks gatherings were the preferred form of entertainment for the self-identified social upper crust in 1950s and '60s Castleton.

In 1960, the Storms were elected co-presidents of the Castleton Historical Society. This was appropriate because status at that time was established by connection to old things: living in an architecturally-meritorious old house, studying Vermont history, belonging to the DAR and the Association of Mayflower Descendents, being knowledgeable about, and often buying and selling, antiques.

Ken Ward, one of the few who remembers much about them, tells me that Ethel was from Middlebury, Eric from Connecticut, and the couple's money came from Ethel's first husband.

Ken says that Ethel is buried in Middlebury, and that Eric wound up in Misty Morn Nursing Home. I don't like to think of that sad end for such a one-time grandee. The Rolls was donated to the Castleton Lions Club and sold by Frank Taggart at his car dealership in Hydeville.

Count Alexandre and Gladys Orlowski were possibly grander than the Storms. They arrived in town in 1960 and moved into the Main Street Langdon house, which prior to them was owned by Mr. and Mrs. French Campell and was thought to be Dake's masterpiece.

Gladys, a Canadian, the Count's second wife, raised and showed corgis. She arrived with eight of the dogs, and her house still has corgi shaped switchplates in all the downstairs rooms.

When the Orlowskis lived in town, there was a state-of-the-art, fully occupied corgi kennel out in back of their house. It was a free-standing building with a poured cement floor, individual stalls, wall heaters, and an enclosed dog run. A mournful corgi cemetery abutted.

Predictably, the Count was an antiques dealer who built an impressive shop with a caretaker's apartment next to the luxurious corgi kennel.

Because the Orlowskis were living in the center of Castleton, they were more involved in town life than the Storms, and the Count was more warm and outgoing than the Colonel.

Sonya Hackel when she moved from Rutland remembers Gladys, wearing a hat and white gloves, coming across the street to visit officially and telling Sonya that, after inspection, she was willing to sponsor her for membership in the Castleton Women's Club.

Gladys was an Episcopalian and attended tiny St. Mark's, but the Polish Count was a devout Catholic with some standing in the larger Vermont church community.

What I remember, and for which I am eternally grateful to him, was his dissuading the Diocese of Burlington from reusing its ultra modern Arlington Church architectural plans when it decided to build a new St. John's in Castleton.

The Count was a traditionalist who was not prepared to get up each morning and see an aesthetically-jarring Catholic place of worship across the street from him at the corner of North Road. I always think of the admittedly quotidian compromise as his greatest contribution to the town.

In the mid-1970s, practical Gladys decided that they should move into more manageable housing, and in 1975 the couple held a disastrous auction.

Although there was a big crowd, and many gawkers, what people found were largely European things which they failed to recognize, appreciate, or on which they wanted to bid.

I always remember that auction because my husband went to it and brought home our present dining room table.

Prices were disastrously low. When the auctioneer called out, "Who will give me five dollars?" (for a Baccarat paperweight) the outraged and despairing Count stepped in and halted the sale.

He and Gladys packed up what was left, turned the house over to its new owners John and Eileen Smart who had four young daughters, and headed for Otterside condominiums in Middlebury.

"Now I go into prison," the Count said. He was dead in two years.

Martha Towers Remembers

L ast week, my Gibbs cousins gathered in East Barnard at the Paige-Gibbs farm for our annual Cousins' Week-end. At some point, my Uncle Gerald's daughter Paige Gibbs handed around a box of old photographs and asked us to identify and take home any we wanted.

I claimed the photo of Uncle Gerald, my mother's twin brother, and Martha Langdon sitting with two other students, a girl and a boy, on the front steps of Woodruff Hall in the early 1930s. I'd become curious about this young couple. I wanted to know who they were.

There were very few men students at the Normal School in the years my parents, uncles, and aunts were there. I remember my mother talking about an Ellis Towne. It occurred to me that this might be him.

I decided it was time to pay a visit to Martha Towers.

Martha Langdon Towers lives, and has lived for the past fifty-or-so years, in an 1800's South Street house painted what old days Castletonians might have called a peculiar shade of green. She has a lot of surrounding shrubbery which untended for decades has gown shaggy and encroaching.

I've known Martha all my life. My parents knew her all their lives; my grandparents knew her parents all their lives.

Martha is 98. She went to high school with my father, and they were at the Normal together. I knew she was more-or-less managing, but that she no longer got out much. She's stopped going to the Federated Church Sundays and to meetings of the Castleton Women's Club.

Martha has two children, Carol, who entered Smith when she was 16, and a son born with mental and physical disabilities. Carol is an engineer in Binghamton, New York. Chris lives at home with his mother.

I remember Chris as a little boy who soothed himself with repetitive behavior. Now in late middle age he's much the same. He croons and sways. But he can endear himself. During my visit, he comes out of the front room, pats me on the head and says "Pretty."

I go see Martha at four in the afternoon, between the shifts of caregivers.

The Gibbs family going 'over Killington mountain' to visit relatives — little Stan and Alma on board. (Gibbs family collection)

Her living room is like a little burrow, the walls painted a brilliant red. The place is crammed with a lifetime's accumulation of books, dolls, and pillows. There is a long line of photos along the top of the open piano. The TV's on.

Martha and I sit down, and I show her the photo I've brought.

"See how neat he looks," says Martha with warm approval. She's zeroed in on my uncle, whom she always liked.

"We look like we could be related, like we could be brother and sister." She thinks this, I conclude, because the two of them are similarly dressed.

"We had a good time together. We had fun. We had Kate Kelly, (who taught English Literature.) We used to sit there with Kate."

Martha's chuckle sounds a little ribald to me. It's hard to ascertain exactly what she thought of Kate Kelly.

Then she looks at the two people I want her to identify.

"That's Al Manning from Rutland and Winifred Taylor. We called her Winnie. She came from over the mountain. She wasn't one of the Pittsford people."

I think how my aunts and uncles always talked about people who "came from over the mountain." Killington was once seen as a real geographic barrier.

I ask for more details.

"We didn't have any social life together," Martha goes on to explain. "Al was a commuter."

I ask if Al and Winifred later taught.

"We all taught," Martha says impatiently, which I knew. I knew that all Normal School graduates taught, or at least taught for awhile. Martha tells me that she has no idea what happened to Al and Winnie later in life.

But my visit has been a success because she's been able to identify these two young Normal School students who would be nearly 100 years old if they were still alive.

However, I'm sure that they're long dead, and that Martha, still sharp, still hearing clearly, still reading without difficulty, is the only one alive.

"I'm a typical 98-year-old person," she crows with a certain manic complacency, but we both know that she's not typical in any way.

Visits can't be very long these days. It's time for me to go, and Martha, for years a Sunday school music leader, moves to her piano and begins to bang out 'The Lord is Good to Me.'

I stay on the couch, turn over the eighty-year-old photo, and write on the back, Al Manning from Rutland and Winifred Taylor from 'over the mountain.'

I can't help but wonder about their lives. Now I know who they were, but I realize that I'll probably never know what happened to them.

The cousins, Claude and Sadie's grandchildren, at the Old Homestead in Castleton Corners the summer of 1960 (the author is in the second row from the bottom farthest right). (Sandra Gibbs Barth photo)

We Are All Our Mothers' Daughters

Beulah Shaw exemplified farm women I saw growing up. She was what most people around Castleton were at one time. Her strengths were the strengths of all the old timers.

Sharp to the end, she died this last July at ninety-five, and I look around and realize that her kind are now pretty much gone. She is missed and mourned by her daughter Lois Ladd who lives behind Castleton's Main Street Federated Church.

Lois carries on her mother's attitudes and ways. She does this because, as I realize this Mothers' Day, we are, whether we like it, or fight it, are resigned to it, or grateful for it, all our mothers' daughters.

Beulah Whittaker was born in Rochester, Vermont in 1914. She grew up with three brothers, graduated from Rochester High School and went to Rutland Business College. In Rutland she met Glen Shaw, and the couple were married in 1933. They left Rutland and went into farming—at that time a viable option for many.

They farmed in Rochester where they had their first four children and moved on to Danby. That's where Lois, the second-to-youngest child, was born. In 1947, they bought a big spread in Benson, on the east side of Route 30, and had the last of their seven children.

The Shaws liked farming, and they were good at it. Beulah always said it was an honest life. Her business school background helped. She knew how to keep books, and she took care of the financial end of things. She dealt with the milk truck deliveries. Lois remembers her father selling two calves for $700 and telling his little daughter to, "take this money in to your mother."

Lois says that her parents expected, and needed to have, their offspring work hard. She remembers her mother doing the laundry with a wringer washer, baking for big family meals, and raising most of their food. Lois took in that on the farm all activities had a purpose.

In the early 1960s, Beulah and her husband were in their seventies, worn-out and used-up. They sold their farm and moved to a house in Castleton on Route 30. Glen had a hip replacement, spent time in the Rutland Hospital and finished his life in Saegars, the Fair Haven nursing home where a great many area old people ended up.

Beulah sold their house on Route 30 to Lois's daughter Lori and her husband Bob Spaulding and moved into Castleton Meadows where she lived for the next ten years. She continued to bake and made rolls for all of her neighbors, delivering them in little plastic baggies.

She worked for years at Coon's Store at Castleton Corners. On their weekly grocery trips, Lois and her husband Ray sometimes picked her up and gave her a ride. After work, she usually walked home down Route 30.

Eventually, she moved to a residence facility in Rutland. Finally, she had a fall and spent the last month of her life in The Pines nursing home.

This is the first spring that Lois's mother can't visit her. This last Christmas was the first Christmas that she didn't make rolls for the family. And she wasn't in Castleton for Easter. Lois's daughter had taken to driving her grandmother to the Congregational Church in Hubbardton Sundays and bringing her back afterward.

At the end of her life, Lois took her mother to doctors' appointments, and she drove her to get groceries. As all daughters do, she finally became the parent.

One day, she asked Beulah if she was afraid to die. "Yes and no," her mother replied. Beulah said that the reason she wasn't afraid of death was because then she could be with her mother and father again and her three children and the one grandson, Lois's son Brian, who had predeceased her.

Lois Ladd's whole life is a reflection of what she learned growing up. She scrubs and sweeps. Her house shines. Her back lawn is lush, her garden full of flowers. In just the way Beulah babysat for Lois's two children, Brian and Lori, Lois helped bring up her two grandchildren while their mother Lori worked.

She and her husband Ray clean the Federated Church. They planted and maintain its flower beds. For the last twenty-five years, she's been director of the Castleton Food Shelf.

Lois grew up hearing "Work hard for what you have. Be honest and fair." Even without hearing it said, she always knew, 'Honor Your Mother.'

She says that if somehow Beulah Shaw could walk through the door this Mothers' Day, Lois's first welcoming action would be to give her a favorite meal—beef, mashed potatoes with plenty of butter, squash and rolls.

We Will Not See
It's Like Again

R aymond Doran's small sad, now abandoned, family farm sits on the backside of Lake Bomoseen at the head of a little valley which runs between two slate ridges. Ray lived here from the beginning when the place boiled up full of his Doran siblings until the end, nearly eight years ago. He had been here alone for nearly a lifetime raising a few cows, baling some hay, and in old age riding an old horse, a little uncertainly, past his summer cottage neighbors, on Avalon Beach Road.

This is a place that was lived in as one lived in 19th century Vermont and earlier still in Ireland. Now that the owner is gone, we will not see its like again.

One of my father's favorite friends was Eddie Doran, Ray's older brother. My father saw a lot of Eddie when we were living in West Castleton.

Eddie had been in the Second World War, and my father liked to tell a story, as I remember it, about how Eddie had been captured and forced to participate in the legendary Bataan Death March, but Eddie had come through.

My black-humor-loving father always laughed telling me that, of course, Eddie could survive a terrible prisoners' death march. Growing up on a West Castleton subsistence farm in the 1930s, a death march was nothing.

Eddie returned home, right back to West Castleton, married vivacious red haired Nancy, had a great many children, worked as a carpenter, and prospered.

His brother Ray was the last sibling left on the Doran farm and wound up owning it. Ray lived there all his life working off-farm as a mail carrier. He had a few cows in his barn. He baled hay.

Another brother, John, who some time ago moved to Burlington, built a summer cottage a little farther up Avalon Beach Road. Ray's sister Catherine Pellegrino lived for a number of years on Main Street in Castleton, but then moved to a lakeshore place across from the farm. Her son Terry lives year round next to his Uncle John.

Eddie's sons—the Dorans run to sons—have houses along the West Castleton State Park Road. Tommy lives near Bomoseen's Point of Pines. Jimmy used to live on Scotch Hill Road. Almost everyone has stayed around, and they've all gone into useful occupations from providing septic tank services to roofing. Joe Doran is a teacher in the Castleton Village School.

For years, the Doran home farm was a source of speculation. What was going to happen here? It seemed it would stay the same forever, a sort of dilapidated place out of 'Brigadoon.' But in February of 2004, Ray died, and Ray had never gotten around to making a will.

The Doran farm has south-facing meadows looking out over the lake. No one failed to realize that although it had never been much of a working farm it could be carved up into desirable locations for expensive lake houses.

Because it was an intestate situation, before the farm could be sold, clear title required that a great many Doran heirs had to be rounded up.

The Rutland Ryan family, long-time summer neighbors, had always hoped to buy the Doran acreage, and had always wanted to move Avalon Beach

The Doran farm. (Pamela Hayes Rehlen photo)

Road from where it is now, closely following the curve of the lake shore in front of cottages, back onto Doran land behind these cottages.

It's hard not to see this as a good idea—at least for the cottage owners. Without the dusty, sometimes busy, road, these places would have sweeping uninterrupted lawns down to the water.

Two weeks ago, an exultant T. R. Ryan came into the Birdseye Diner to announce that the estate had been settled, and he'd fulfilled his and his father's long-time dream and had bought the Doran farm.

Now there's a further development. Ray Knutsen, the veterinarian owner of Champlain Valley Vineyards in Benson, last week bought fifty-five acres of the Doran farmland. Although this is thin, slatey soil, it's lakeside acreage, and lakeside acreage, for both orchards and vineyards, is the best acreage of all.

For awhile, the Doran Farm stays as it's always been. The barbed wire fence is open next to St. Matthew's Church which was a one-time Doran barn and the family's long-ago gift to the Vermont Catholic Diocese.

The doors to the farmhouse are also open, both rain and wind come in. A porch addition is now a pile of debris. The barn's cow stalls are empty and littered with trash. A farm track leads up past a weathered stile under an apple tree to a moonscape of slate exploration and a water-filled quarry hole.

Right now, everything is quiet and abandoned and sad, poignant and backward-looking. Ray is planning on burning the buildings, but presently this little place is just as Ray Doran left it.

When it's gone, and it will soon be gone, we will not see its like again.

The Vermonter
Who Came Home

S tan Gibbs never forgot going down Sunday mornings before dawn into the Castleton Federated Church cellar which smelled of old stone and kerosene and coal ash. Stan's younger brother Gerald, still in high school, had a job starting the furnace, and although Stan and Gerald would have been out all night at a dance, they always got back in time and got the furnace going and soon had the church interior warmish.

When first sunshine was buttering the deep snow's crusted surface, Stan and Gerald came up out of the cellar. On mornings when it was 20 below, smoke from the houses on Main Street rose straight up, and the air was so sharp that it pinched Stan's nose.

The brothers wore Adirondack trapper-style greatcoats and on their heads black toques. Stan never forgot that still, frigid, well-known world and the comfort of his brother and him walking along easy and close, their gaitered boots making creaking sounds on the bone dry snow.

Stan Gibbs moved away from Vermont, to Massachusetts, in 1939 to work in the Watertown Arsenal. He stayed away for thirty-five years. He always wanted, and he finally managed, to get back to the place from which he'd come.

He was born August 28, 1910 on a farm at the Castleton end of the East Hubbardton Road to Claude and Sadie Fish Gibbs. Stan was their second child and first son. The Gibbses were part of a clan of successful Hubbardton hill farmers.

Stan's great-great-grandfather Nathan Gibbs had moved from eastern Massachusetts to Pittsford, Vermont in the 1790s and came to own the Pittsford Iron Works.

Nathan's grandson Byron Delos Gibbs, who was born in 1850, moved to, and farmed successfully enough in Hubbardton to be able to go to the legislature and build a showplace house on Monument Hill Road.

At a time Stan remembered well, Gibbses owned, in contiguous farms, most of the land in Hubbardton from Hubbardton Gulf to Giddings Brook to Sargent Hill and down Monument Hill Road to the Turnpike School.

Byron Delos's oldest son Claude, Stan's father, who Stan loved deeply and all his life emulated, farmed during the warm weather months on land below his own father's place on Monument Hill Road.

In order to make it easier for his six children to go to school, Claude moved his family into rented houses—most on Main Street in Castleton—during the wintertime.

At some point, Claude Gibbs got a government job, carrying mail on the rugged thirty-mile Hubbardton mail route, a great piece of good fortune which provided him with a secure occupation all through the Depression and for the rest of his working life. He continued to farm on the side.

His son Stan graduated from West Rutland High School in June 1927 when he was sixteen. At graduation, Stan stood about five foot two. Later, when he reached his full height, he favored his mother's tall, long-boned Fish relatives and became a formidably large and powerful man. After high school, unlike his siblings, he didn't continue his education at 'The Normal' in Castleton. He wanted no part of teaching.

Stan wanted to farm. He went up to Hubbardton to the land his father was working. He herded cows, and he drew wood down to Castleton. He did every kind of odd job, but by the 1920s there was no future in hill farming.

The young Claude Gibbs family with Alma, Stan and baby Connie. (Gibbs family collection)

Stan signed up for an apprentice machinist program at the General Electric plant in Schenectady. Over the next few years, he was sent briefly to Pennsylvania, and he worked in the Jones and Lambert machine shop in Springfield, Vermont. Most weekends, he managed to get home to help out his mother and father.

In January 1939, Stan heard that the Arsenal in Watertown, just outside of Boston, was hiring. He borrowed his younger brother Gerald's car and drove to Massachusetts. "Can you start this afternoon?" they asked him. He said he could, and he moved into a boarding house down the street from the plant.

The following summer, July 1939, Stan married Ruth Seward, his childhood neighbor on the East Hubbardton Road and his playmate at the Castleton Elementary School.

In 1949, after their two children were born, Ruth and Stan moved into a small Cape Cod style house at 101 Fordham Road in West Newton, Massachusetts.

The years went by. When the Arsenal closed in 1965, Stan worked awhile longer as a machinist on the Cambridge Electron Accelerator, a shared Harvard University, M. I. T. project, and at the tool shop at Mass. General Hospital.

He retired in 1974 when he was sixty-four years old. With their Castleton Normal School degrees, all his brothers and sisters had moved out of state to teach. Now, they were planning on retiring to Florida.

The summer of 1975, his younger brother and he, as they had for the last twenty-five years, rented a cottage so their families could be together on the west side of Lake Bomoseen.

Stan drove into Castleton and he saw at the end of Main Street that the Ed Ellis house had a For Sale sign out on the front lawn. Stan knew this place. He came back to the cottage on the lake, and he told his siblings how well built the house was.

"We know that, Stan," they said.

His brothers and sisters wanted to talk about retiring to Florida to play golf, and Stan wanted to talk about the old days at home with Mother and Dad, about Dad's mail route.

When Claude first started carrying the mail up into Hubbardton, he drove two horses. Stan, always responsible and protective of Claude, had himself made an official Substitute Mail Carrier, and he sometimes rode with his father.

On the worst winter days, the East Hubbardton Road was plowed only enough to allow passage for Claude's sleigh. Neighbors along the route waited, and if their mailman hadn't arrived by a certain time, they went out to find him and dig him out of the deep snow.

To make it easier for the horses, Stan got out and walked the loop road below the East Hubbardton Cemetery and would meet his father farther along the way. Claude heated in the stove at home a brick until it was red hot and put this brick into his mail sleigh on a tray under a buffalo skin robe.

The heat from this foot-warmer-arrangement comforted him most of the day. People along the route who needed to buy stamps put out change in metal trays which on well-below-zero days, when he tried to scoop the money out, froze to a mailman's hand.

When Claude had replaced his horses with an auto, he drove over the snow with tire chains, and in the cold and on the rough terrain of the winter roads, the chains would break and the links snap and flap.

If Stan and his brother Gerald were riding with him, Claude asked, "Aren't you going to fix that chain?" But when it was 35 below with the wind whipping along Eaton Hill and the route ahead nearly a tunnel through the deep snow, the sons came back silent in the face of their father's question, "Were you able to mend it?"

That summer in 1975 at the rented cottage on Lake Bomoseen, Stan was restless, free after his lifetime's work. He sat out on the deck and talked about Mother and Dad. He talked about the Langdon wood lot and ice fishing on Bomoseen. He talked about breaking the roads in Hubbardton and driving his grandfather's cows to pasture.

"That's all changed now, Stan." his brothers and sisters told him. "It isn't like that around here any more."

At the end of the August rental, as everyone was packing up to head home, Stan drove down to the Riley Agency and arranged to buy the Ellis House. Stan had always had money. He was thrifty and saving. He made a big cash down payment, and then he and Ruth went back to Massachusetts to dispose of 101 Fordham Road.

⌂⌂⌂

In a whirlwind of reconnections, Stan came home. He went on what for him was a buying spree. He bought a Rototiller, a black and silver Arctic Cat snowmobile. He had Ed Ellis's old furnace hauled away and a new top-of-the-line model installed.

"You don't need to do that, Stan," someone said, but Stan replied, "I don't want to take any chances. It gets cold here winters. It goes down to 30 below sometimes. I remember once," and he was off talking about Mother and Dad, their long-ago trials and old-fashioned satisfactions that had never paled for Stan.

He wanted to help. He wanted to take charge as he always had at home. He was local now. A Mason all his life, first going to meetings with his father on the second floor of the brick Masonic building in the center of Castleton, Stan had become a Shriner and had been a member of the Aleppo Temple in Boston, part of their marching patrol. Now he joined Rutland's Cairo Temple. He rejoined his old Masonic Lodge which met upstairs over the Riley Agency. Ruth rejoined the Eastern Star.

Ruth and Stan walked across the street to the Federated Church. In the pearly gray church interior, Stan sat in the Gibbs pew against the sanctuary's east wall, just behind the window that looked out over the town's earliest graveyard, and Ruth went up back and sang with the choir.

Renting on the lake was a thing of the past. Stan turned to real, year-round life. In the spring, he arranged to have his house repainted. He had the roof fixed. He laid out where his garden would be, just like Claude's, an acre of vegetables with a little tool shed.

Stan's land ran all the way back to the railroad tracks that went south to Poultney. He talked about getting chickens. He said he'd really like a cow too, but Ruth became fierce at the mention of keeping a cow. Stan bought an army surplus parka with fur around the face, the kind worn by scientists who man mountain-top weather stations.

That fall, Stan sat in his Laz-Z-Boy chair watching the television weather forecasts and like an eager bridegroom waited for winter. Each morning, he walked down Main Street to the Castleton Village Store to get milk and the paper.

The fall grew darker; the trees became black and barren, and a cold wind whipped down Main Street and swirled dead, unraked leaves. Finally, winter came. Some mornings, it was well below zero. Snow was threatening or a Travelers' Advisory was in effect. Other dark mornings, it was snowing heavily, slowing the few cars along Main Street to a crawl.

Sometimes when Stan arrived—at this point in his life a big man with bowed legs, a farmer's barrel chest and long powerful arms, the store radio would be predicting a bitter night ahead, temperatures of 15 below, a wind chill factor of minus thirty.

Stan stamped across the old store's wet and road-salt-dirty wooden floor to the cast iron chunk stove.

"I recall at home Dad would stoke this up until it glowed red," Stan said to his cousin Rus Fish who was often standing around ready to talk about the old days.

"He couldn't get it hot enough because he was going out with the mail and he didn't know what he'd encounter or when he'd get home. I remember once when I was riding with Dad the snow was so deep we were in a tunnel all the way to the Parsons sisters."

Stan's voice rang out confident, loud, and happy, talking about the old things and the old times. Stan Gibbs had come home.

Ed Ryan's 100th Birthday Party

For years now when I've driven by his house, I've worried about how Ed Ryan was faring. He was a boyhood friend of my father's. My father was born October 25, 1911, and Ed was born February 16, 1912.

The two of them were Fair Haven school mates. In those days Ed was 'Porky' Ryan. This sobriquet must have come out of some now-forgotten town misadventure. No Fair Haven youth of that era went without a nickname.

But it turns out, during all those drive-bys, that I didn't need to worry about Ed. Although my father died four years ago at ninety-six, Ed continues to go strong, and on February 20th, he had a 100th birthday party given by family and friends up at the Trak Inn.

The day was bright and cold. It felt like spring was on the way; the lake ice looked a little dodgy. Ed arrived with his daughter Kathy Ryan who lives in Colorado Springs and works for Sbar Construction on the Pearson Air Force Base. She's been out in Colorado since 1973, but she returns to Vermont for two to three weeks every summer to see her father.

The other two people who got Ed to the Trak Inn, Ed now using a walker because he says "I have no balance at all," were Jim Foley, Ed's sister's son, up from Vero Beach for this celebration, and John 'Downsey' Burke, trusted *consigliore* to the area 'Old Irish.'

Ed Ryan at his 100th birthday party. (Pamela Hayes Rehlen photo)

Downsey recounted how, as a boy, he used to run up to Nesto's to do errands for Mr. and Mrs. Ryan. (I have a warm spot in my heart for anyone who remembers Nestos little grocery store.)

For this centennial birthday party, Ed was looking good. He had on a sharp suit from Rutland's McNeil and Reedy and a Knights of Columbus lapel pin. His nephew Jim told me that at one time Ed had been the oldest serving Knight of Columbus.

Kathy Ryan said that, through word of mouth, about a hundred people had been invited to this party. It looked like most had taken Ed up on his invitation.

The Trak Inn tables were full and festooned with birthday balloons. Next to Ed, there was a cake ordered by Peggy Green, a birthday greeting from the president, and a Papal Blessing.

The Papal Blessing seemed like something well-earned. Ed was long time treasuer, and kept the accounts, for Castleton's St. John's Catholic Church. Now, John Burke brings the Eucharist to him at home every week.

Ed's life's work was with the Delaware and Hudson Railroad Line, initially as a telegraph operator, later, as an accountant and bursar. He's an old railroad man.

He worked for the D and H for, "forty-four years and six months." As a result, he lived in Albany for thirty years, where, as John Burke tells me *sotto voce*, Ed was the friend of bishops and mayors.

Then he returned to Vermont with his wife Josephine—Jo—to the house where he lives now, where he was born, and in which he hopes to die.

For years, he and Jo sat out on the front porch and watched the cars go by. This is a time-honored activity at Castleton Corners. My grandparents did the same thing. Jo died in 1994, and then Ed sat out alone.

I remember this vigorous man when he was in his eighties, smoking a cigar and shooting around Castleton in the Grande Marquis Mercury that he reluctantly sold in 1997.

He last ran into my father up at the Wheel Restaurant in Benson. The Wheel was originally a livery stable—that's something they both would have known. As a boy, my father took my grandfather's horses there to be shod.

Now, in his hundredth year, Ed gets up around eight. He reads the paper, for years it was the Albany Times Union. His nephew Jim says his uncle stays active all day. He talks on the phone to his daughter Kathy. He watches the news on television and uses a computer. He still figures his taxes, writes letters, handles his finances, and pays his bills

Peggy Green comes by daily, often with her two pretty, grown daughters, to see what he needs and to generally help out. Pete Heilig, the Hydeville Post master, stops by every evening to check again and bring him his mail.

Today, the birthday guests just keep coming through the door.

"Hi there, Mr. Ed. You're handsome as ever."

"Keep on going, Kiddo. I miss seeing you in church. I miss seeing you in the Price Chopper."

"Did you eat that apple pie I brought you all by yourself?"

My favorite greeting: "How ya feeling. You don't look a day over ninety-nine."

Ed says, "All my friends and family are here."

He's happy, but getting tired because interacting with a room packed with people, trading jokes and stories, politely asking about friends' families, is quite an undertaking when you're a hundred years old.

The Allen Brothers—
Still in the Game

Only four Castleton farms are still sending their milk out on the Dairy Farmers of America trucks to East Greenwich, New York. They're Ransomvale Farm, the Harris Farm, the Traverse Farm, and the farm operated by the Allen brothers.

You have to take your hat off to them. Corn silage used to sell for one hundred dollars an acre. Presently, thanks to the drought out West, corn silage goes for fifteen hundred dollars an acre.

Right now is, as Bobby Allen says, "a bad time to be farming."

Sometimes, you wonder if there was ever any good time. Maybe three years ago when the price of milk was high and the price of grain reasonable. But that's the way it is. Vermont farming is, and always has been, a tough business.

Of the four still-operating Castleton dairy farms, the Allen operation is in some ways the most unique. This is the home place of a band of seven siblings, four brothers in the house, one brother down the road, two sisters close by.

Bobby Allen in his cow barn. (Pamela Hayes Rehlen photo)

The Allens own two hundred acres of river bottom on the East Hubbardton Road. Fifty-three-year old Bobby, the middle Allen, says that there are too many rocks and some clay, but otherwise his family place "grows good crops."

By that he means hay and corn. He says in addition to what they raise they have to buy high protein feed from Depot Farm Supply in Leister.

The Allens have 160 to 170 cows. They milk 80. This is a small herd by today's standards, but they're able to send off 6,500 pounds of milk every other day on the DFA truck which rumbles up the East Hubbardton Road from Castleton to receive a much larger daily product from much larger Ransomvale Farm.

All the Allen brothers but Harold work 'off farm,' and this is what allows them to stay in business. Bobby has been getting up each morning at 3:30 for the last four years and driving to the Milborne Farm on the Richville Dam Road in Shoreham to work as morning milker. He used to be employed by the O'Rourkes.

For the last thirty-five years, Bobby's brother David has been delivery man for S. E. Smith Farm Supply in West Rutland. His brother Randy is a handyman on a beef spread in Brandon. Ronnie Allen is down the road at Ransomvale Farm.

There are two Allen sisters. Linda works in Castleton doing billing for Sid Waite. She's one of the three siblings who isn't living at home, but she's close by in a new house she built on Allen land.

Patty Cook lives in Hydeville. Her two sons, Shawn and Justin come up for night chores and plan to eventually take over their uncles' business.

The Allen operation—which looks like it's been around forever, and which anyone would imagine the Allens have owned forever—is actually a fairly new establishment.

Howard and Eva Lawrence Allen came originally from Shrewsbury, where their families had always farmed, and bought the Castleton place, which had been lying idle, in the mid 1960s. Bobby thinks that his parents paid $60,000—an enormous sum for that time.

Eva died in 1979 and Howard in 1992. The original farmhouse burned down in a woodstove fire twenty-two years ago, and now four of the Allen sons live together in a modern house across the road from their barn.

Only two Allens—David and Patty—have ever married. This allows for a powerful focus on the family business. No one takes anything out of the operation. Any profit—and these days there isn't much profit—gets put back into the farm, for example to purchase a really good cow for breeding or to buy a better piece of equipment.

Many would find this an unacceptably marginal way to live, but as Bobby says, laughing, "We're all still here, so it must be working."

Bobby graduated from Fair Haven Union High school in 1977. He never considered anything but farm work. It was more than familiar; to him it was also a meaningful way of life.

He says about being home in the mornings, "It's a zoo. We'll pass each other as we all go out to our jobs."

It's probably a comforting chaos, one that these men have experienced all of their lives. Now in middle age, it's just as it once was in high school.

Living with very little money and working harder than most people can imagine, Bobby sits out in a lawn chair by the barn and says of his existence, "On a farm, you just don't worry about things."

I suggest that with bulk milk and grain prices where they are now maybe one might worry about the source of their next meal.

Bobby laughs at my cynicism, then cheerfully deflects it by referring to the Birdseye which he visits every day and where he has a wide circle of friends.

"No, as long as the diner's open, I'll *always* find a next meal.

The Past is
a Different Country

The Castleton Federated Church was built in 1833, the next door, one-time Langdon house, now the Watermans', in 1800. The Higley House down the street was built in 1811, our house, the Manse, in the 1840s. Castleton is an old town. It's 250th birthday was September 22nd.

On a glorious summer day fifteen or twenty years ago, I remember being in a ruminative mood, wondering what it would have really been like to live long ago, for example when Castleton was a brand new town.

I knew that this area was first visited by the surveyors Noah Lee and Amos Bird in 1766. Amos Bird climbed Birdseye Mountain for a better view of his surroundings. Later, he took a house lot on the west side of the new Castleton village, and Lee claimed his house lot close to the river on Castleton's east side.

But none of what they may have built, or where they once lived, still stands.

Thirsting for 'felt history,' I sat on my front porch and looked out at Main Street, which must have been the same east- west thoroughfare that Lee and

Bird knew and that they had probably laid out.

Across Main Street, the Federated Church graveyard was also early, not going back to the 1760s, but early. I went over and wandered among the gravestones trying to imagine this town's first settlers, many of whom died young in this place where I now lived and with which I strongly identified.

After a while, I returned and sat next to a pillar on the east side of the Manse, where no one ever sits.

The Manse has been a bustling place all of its life, largely because of its being, first, a center-of-things showplace, and later a center-of-things church parsonage.

But when we bought the house, we gave up a common driveway, and that meant the east-side front door was no longer convenient. Finally, in the best old time Vermont tradition, we stopped using both of the front doors.

So, I sat there in a part of the Manse porch where no one had sat for years, and all of a sudden—on this still, empty, brilliantly-sunny day—I saw what seemed to be vast clouds of smoke billowing up from behind the Federated Church graveyard.

This wasn't coming from the Beacon Feeds Mill, at that time still in operation. It surged and billowed higher. It filled the sky. It wasn't a fire. What was this great outpouring of not-smoke? Finally, it stopped billowing. It thinned and drifted off. The town seemed deserted. I went into the house. I made some calls, to the fire station, to the town hall. No one had seen it.

I never found out what it was. It came to symbolize for me everything on which we can't get a handle. And I've come to realize that one of the things on which we can't get a handle is a visceral sense of the past.

Thursday, September 22nd, Castleton had a little party to commemorate its 250th birthday. Castleton is one of fourteen Rutland County towns, including Killington, Pawlet, Danby, Mt. Tabor, Shrewsbury, Clarendon, Rutland Town, Tinmouth, Wells, Pittsford, Brandon, Wallingford and Poultney, which turn 250 this year. Poultney is celebrating with fireworks, a parade, and clowns.

Holly Hitchcock, president of the Castleton Historical Society, said that she didn't feel she could come close to matching Poultney's celebration—and where were all those Poultney volunteers coming from anyway?

But she confidently predicted that she wouldn't be around for Castleton's three hundredth birthday, and so decided she had to do something.

This was good news to Linda Pritchard, the incoming president of the Castleton Woman's Club, who announced Holly's plans at the club's fall luncheon.

The Historical Society's Higley House was open September 22nd from 3 to 5, with a birthday party going on the same time as, just down the street, the weekly Thursday afternoon Castleton Farmers' Market.

A cake had been ordered up. Local artist Marna Grove, who teaches at the college and lives out on Pencil Mill Road, created a birthday cake sign. Claire Burditt, town historian, wrote up a history fact sheet which was sent home tucked into local students' school packets.

Holly Hitchcock, Castleton Historical Society president, standing at the door of the Higley House at the time of the town's 250th 'birthday.' (Pamela Hayes Rehlen photo)

The author's grandparents, far left, Mary and Burness Hayes at an evening social in West Haven, Vermont. After hearing a mildly risqué double entendre, the ladies are stifling a laugh. (Hayes family collection)

Sexton Ray Ladd climbed to the steeple at 3 p.m. and rang the Federated Church bells two hundred and fifty times. Ray is a meticulous, plan-ahead guy, and he'd calculated that it would take him seven minutes.

I looked forward to Ray's ringing of the bells. I walked down to the Higley House and had a piece of cake, and I imagined how bemused our beleaguered Castleton forebears, locavors all, often by desperate necessity, would have been to see the much-promoted, much-toiled-over, farmers' market.

We can celebrate our past as we imagine it to be. We can bake it a birthday cake, but I don't think we can ever really feel it and know it, because as I learned so long ago sitting on my porch, it's a mystery. The past is a different country.

Heatwave

It's been in the 80s, 90s, near 100, a lot lately. The Fourth of July was a long, sweltering, perfect-summer week-end. When it's this hot, every day feels like a day off, the summer equivalent of a school-closings snow day. It can be brutal, but it's a special time of year.

The Ragazzi Boys' Chorus from San Francisco came to Castleton Friday night and ran up and down the narthex stairs and sat in the balcony and filled the Federated Church, which hasn't been filled like this in years.

The boys sang selections from Handel, Schumann, and Schubert and then, near the end of the program, the whole fresh-faced, blue-blazer-wearing, sixty-member group spread out around the church interior, close to the perspiring, enthusiastic audience, and danced and sang 'Put a Little Love in Your Heart' and selections from ABBA. I can't remember the church being that exhilaratingly-full of people and of energy since, maybe, sometime in the 1950s.

Afterward, the deaconate set up long tables on the front lawn and served the performers and the audience cookies and cakes and make-your-own sundaes. Much later, the little boys, now in T shirts and shorts, ran back and forth around the town green close to the church graveyard letting off steam, their shouts echoing in the hot humid darkness.

The next morning, early, the Saturday before the 4th, my husband and I bike to Fair Haven in order to make a big loop around by the lake. We pass my grandmother's house on Dutton Avenue and head up Scotch Hill where, when I was a girl, the 'Blind Boys' used to have their primitive last-century farmstead. Now, there's no evidence of their place, and trim new houses line this road.

We continue past reopened slate quarries, which I remember sitting abandoned and silent. We start coasting down the long hill past the one-time Roberts farmhouse, burned and gone.

Trees now block a spectacular view west into New York State and the Adirondack high peaks. When my family went on summer visits to my grandmother's, I used to ride in the back seat of our car, behind my mother, my head thrust out the window into a rush of hot wind. At that time, there were no trees and I was able to see for miles.

My husband and I reach Glen Lake. We pass and hail Jim Doran who is standing with a group of people on the doorstep of a lakeside Larkin cottage. When we were children, Jimmy and I lived close to each other in West Castleton, and he and his two sisters and my sister swam and played together. Our parents went around together. Now, on this hot summer morning in 2010, we're both in West Castleton again.

The road continues downhill through where a slate village once stood, little quarry workers' houses long collapsed, lost in stands of sumac and box alder. Years ago, my father drove this, then dirt road, three times a day to get to his job as head waiter on the other side of the lake at the Prospect House Hotel.

My husband and I begin clicking through our bike gears, laboring up a long steep hill past newly-built Doran houses. These are Jim's brothers. Almost all the many Doran offspring stayed close to where they grew up on the back side of the lake, and all have done well for themselves. Farther on, I go past tiny clearings in the woods which I remember as little hardscrabble buildings, now long disappeared.

The road heads down hill again, then hugs the western shore of Bomoseen. Not a cloud in the sky, the sun is blindingly bright, and because it's still early in the morning, the air smells strongly of lake water and boat gasoline. I know that soon the day will be humid and stifling, but now it's fresh and bright and full of promise.

The next day is the Fourth of July, and the heat wave continues. Little flags flutter all along Castleton's Main Street. I get up early and see women coming along putting them into place. I feel like I'm spying on Santa Claus filling Christmas stockings.

I remember the year I first saw these flags. It was very early on another bright hot Fourth of July. I was driving in from our cottage, and there they were. They started along the road in Hydeville, marched around the Hydeville green, continued down Route 4, through Castleton Corners and past the Homestead. They started up again in Castleton, all along Main Street, seemingly miles of little bright dancing flags.

It took my breath away.

The Freshman Walk

When I walk very early September mornings on Castleton's South Street a memory always comes back to me. It's the memory of the first time I realized, about a happening in my life, "This is important. This I will never forget."

Fifty years ago, on a hot, end-of-summer Sunday afternoon, a day before freshman week was to begin, my parents left me off at Castleton State Teachers' College.

My mother and father had both gone to Castleton, and as I remember, they were totally off-hand about the place, and asked, and had no trouble arranging, to leave me a day early in a seemingly-empty, unsupervised dorm.

We just drove up the hill with my stuff, including my high school graduation gift, a portable Remington typewriter, and lavender Bates bedspread and curtains which my mother and I had chosen earlier in the summer at Rutland's Economy Department Store.

I was worried about arriving at school a day early and bitterly disappointed with the lack of fanfare attendant on my going off to college. But my parents didn't think going up to CSC—still thought of by them, and almost everyone else, as The Normal—was a big deal.

They said, "It's more convenient if we drop you off today."

My mother found the room assigned to me in Leavenworth Hall, the older and smaller of the college's two women's dorms. Ellis Hall, which housed one hundred and twenty six girls, was out on South Street.

Sixty girls lived in Leavenworth, a massive brick building that I would have thought was indestructible. But ten years later, one cold midwinter night, Leavenworth Hall burned to the ground.

My Leavenworth dormitory was next door to Woodruff Hall, CSC's administration building. The two places were connected by a little covered walkway, which ran right below the open window of the room to which I'd been assigned.

The following week, when students arrived and classes started, I could hear and see almost everything that was happening on that walkway. I particularly appreciated this close-by bustle because the roommate assigned to me decided at the last minute that she wasn't coming to college.

Also, months later, when as a disciplinary action I was room-campused for a week—I was by then going out with a student from Whitehall and had returned to the dorm on more than one occasion three minutes late—my proximity to this social crossroads made my room a lively and interesting place in which to be locked up.

However, that first afternoon in my new dorm-home, room campusing was unimaginable. I put clothes in my closet, set out photographs of my family, and made up my bed with the new lavender spread.

Finally, I went out into the corridor, which was dim and dusty and silent. All the hall doors were topped with transoms, like offices in 1930's detective novels. I wandered into a centrally-located bathroom with a row of lavatory stalls and showers.

Afternoon sun flooded in through screened, west-facing windows. I sat down on the floor under one of the open windows, and in a melancholy state of mind, listened to steady late-summer insect buzz.

My parents had dropped me off on September 10th about one o'clock Sunday afternoon. Freshman orientation was scheduled for Wednesday, with regular school classes beginning at 8 o'clock on Thursday. My parents had been told that a few upperclassmen working on orientation might be around at some point.

After finding my room and helping me lug my few possessions up the stairs to pile on my bed, my mother and father had taken my younger sister and me to the B and B Diner, which at that time was a big place behind tall pines out in Hydeville.

They bought me a substantial meal. I didn't come from a family of coddlers. That B. and B. feed was intended to carry me over until whenever the school began to serve meals.

▲▲▲

The next day, Monday morning, for the English placement test that I was comfortably sure I was going to ace, I got up at seven and walked across campus to the school gym. This gym was more evidence of CSC's recent growth and progress. It had been built two years earlier on the site of the one-time estate of Castleton native son and railroad magnate George Ellis.

When I left the gym—I later learned that I had in fact aced English Placement—I decided to head back across campus and investigate the college library, at that time a large, two-level room reached through French doors off Woodruff Hall's busy, noisy lobby.

Several tables were on the library's upper level, but later, when the school year started, I saw few students sitting there. The library's not-very-extensive stacks were at the western end of the large room, and a fireplace was at the eastern end. Next to the fireplace, there was a little reading area where I found a dusty stack of French language *Paris Match* magazines.

During the two years that I was at CSC, I never remember using the school library for any research purposes, but I went in regularly to look—my French wasn't up to puzzling out much of the text—at *Paris Match's* thrillingly cosmopolitan photographs.

▲▲▲

Monday afternoon was when I had a definite feeling that there might be others on the island, and my Robinson Caruso dorm life could be coming to an end. I was sure I heard distant, tiny voices, and I decided on some dorm exploration. I crept upstairs.

Anyone could see that Leavenworth's third floor was nicer, although the lay out of the second and third floors was identical. The third floor views were better, and with higher ceilings, it was airier. As I moved timidly forward, I realized that the voices I'd heard were coming from a gloriously light-filled, southwest, corner room. The door was open.

It was a big deal for me to walk boldly through the door, like jumping into deep, dark water, but I did it because my parents, over our B. and B. Diner lunch, had prepared me for this sort of unavoidable challenge, had stressed that college life in the main was no bowl of cherries, but assured me that bold initiative always paid off.

I came into a room of startled upperclassmen who when they saw me fell silent. Castleton was a tiny school. Five-hundred-and-six were enrolled that year, up from three-hundred-and-eighty-nine the year before. Total dorm capacity was two hundred and sixteen. With these kinds of numbers, all faces were familiar, but no one had ever seen me, and incoming freshman weren't supposed to be here yet.

When I came through the door, I was looking straight at the absolute leader of the upperclassmen pack, a tiny raven-haired extrovert—I'll call her

Gloria—who was Leavenworth Hall dorm president and all-around student powerhouse.

In the manner of that era when kids emulated adults, she had created for herself in this dorm a home away from home with braided rugs, bookcases, a rocking chair and a crucifix on the wall over her big confectionary nest of a bed.

Gloria wasn't a leader for nothing. In a second, she sized me up and thrust forward a poinsettia-decorated tin box filled with brownies. Her girls rustled apart and rearranged themselves, making a place for me on Gloria's blinding-white, organdy flounced, bedspread.

"We're just getting caught up, finding out who got engaged over the summer," Gloria explained.

As well as brownies, Gloria's girls were holding thick green bottles of coke, purchased from a red and white soda machine I found several days later, humming gently in the perpetual twilight of the Leavenworth Hall basement.

I was saved. These brownies would tie me over, and I learned that the dining hall would be open that night for dinner. Some of Gloria's girls had to change into waitress uniforms and round up their white nurse's shoes and hairnets. They were headed for Leavenworth Hall's cavernous basement kitchen, which was the workplace, also, of the large and capable women pastry cooks who had just finished up their summer jobs at Lake Bomoseen's Prospect House Hotel.

Once her girls were gone, Gloria found her knitting and curled up against the many pillows of her sumptuous bed ready to learn all she could about me.

▲▲▲

Gloria decided to introduce me to her friends who were upperclassmen and campus movers and shakers. She had a boyfriend who I don't remember well, but I'll never forget her best friends (whose names I've changed,) tiny ponytailed, Erin, the Ellis dorm president, and Howie, Erin's psychotically-posses-sive boyfriend. Erin and Howie were continually brawling sweethearts.

When I started at Castleton, the legal drinking age in New York State was eighteen, and everyone's social life revolved around trips "over the line" to the less than ten miles away Hampton Manor bar.

I'd never had a drink in my life and wanted to keep it that way, but I wasn't uncomfortable sitting around with drinkers, so later when everyone left for Hampton Manor to socialize, Gloria arranged for me to come along.

▲▲▲

The next morning, Tuesday, at 7 a.m. I had more tests scheduled in the gym. Besides Glenbrook Gym, CSC at that time had only about seven buildings: Leavenworth Hall, Woodruff Hall, the old Medical School Building which stood next to Woodruff and, we were told, was borderline unsafe for occu-pancy. But still, this is where, later in the year, I met as part of music profes-sor Bob Aborn's small singing group.

There was also the Science Building, Ellis Hall, Dr. Sokolow's tiny astro-nomical observatory on the northernmost edge of the campus, where the cam-pus started to become farm fields, and Dr. Dundas's residence, Phillips House, a tree shaded old place with a barn—the original Leavenworth farm house.

I walked past all of these buildings on my return from testing in the gym. I also remember three college parking lots, one in front of Leavenworth, one in front of Ellis, and one on the north side of Glenbrook Gym. None of these lots ever had many cars in them—although the majority of students at CSC at that time were commuters from Rutland.

A dance was scheduled for Tuesday night, but I decided to pass it up. I retreated to my room, pushed the second bed that no roommate was coming to occupy into a far corner, typed a letter home, smoked a Salem from a little sample pack handed out in the cafeteria the day before, and settled down to read a Rex Stout mystery.

As the evening went on, I'd stop reading every few minutes and study Woodruff Hall's dark windows. The few cars still parked out in front of Leavenworth drove away. Finally, I put the Rex Stout down, opened my transom-topped door and walked out into the hall. The whole silent, old fashioned, solidly-constructed dormitory was deserted and full of shadows.

▲▲▲

I woke up because the fire alarm was ringing and people were running and shouting. My room was cold and black. Someone was hammering on my door, calling, "Get dressed. Meet in the bathroom."

Which is what I did. I'd noted earlier that the bathroom was a big room. And now there were lots of new faces in there, apprehensive faces. Gloria was up on a chair, surrounded by her lieutenants, and she was saying that initiation had begun!

Upset, confused, some not fully awake, Leavenworth freshmen were herded toward the stairs, and then we were down the stairs in a wild scramble and outside through the fire exit door, corralled close to Miss Moriarity's lilac bushes. Howie, along with the other boys who weren't allowed to come into the girls' dorm, was waiting for us with his girlfriend Erin.

Howie—always on a low boil, because Erin was so indiscriminately flirtatious and he so possessive—took charge. In boot camp style, he shouted, "Alright people, let's move out."

He'd been in the service and was at Castleton on the G. I. Bill. During my time, this was true for a number of older men at CSC.

Freshmen were arranged in a ragged walking line. Upperclassmen sat behind the wheel of a few cars. Finally, we were grouped to the initiators' satisfaction. We started off, down the path past Miss Moriarity's little red house, onto South Street, past Ellis Hall, over the railroad tracks. Fields were now on either side of us; night blackness was slipping away like smoke.

Word traveled along the line that we were on a five-mile hike. We were outraged and disbelieving. Could they do this? Was it legal?

The sun was coming up, the village of Castleton left behind. Mist hung above the low fields and marshy places of one-time Leavenworth farm. Little bright birds hopped on telephone wires, perched on silvery fence posts, chirped and whistled at the slow cars patrolling our long ragged line.

A black thunderbird headed up our parade with Howie and Erin lounging on the hood. Howie shouted taunts, lunged forward to beat his hands on the car hood, and then returned to Erin's embrace.

All of this should have been arduous and humiliating. But as I said, I came to a profound realization that morning.

As we marched steadily into the Indian Summer day that was opening like the petals of a golden flower, the sun now warm on our backs, mist lifting and thinning, I saw the South Street Chesborough and Blackwood farms with their gentle meadows and sturdy little 1940's hay silos as a vision of pastoral continuity.

I knew what I was experiencing was something exhilarating that I would never get to experience again because it was part of an intensely-impressionable time in my life which would never occur again.

And I knew that I would always remember it.

The Jimmy Lynch House

Early Sunday morning they burned down the Jimmy Lynch house. This not-very-special little wooden building was in the very center of the Castleton State College campus. In the 1970s, Jimmy Lynch lived there with his family and worked in town as a carpenter. It was a place with dogs and a garden and maybe chickens, where life was lived in that self sufficient way life was lived in a small Vermont town up through the Second World War and beyond.

The college, initially the Normal School, surrounded the Lynch house. The school wasn't much of a place, and little changed there from year to year. A number of students wanting to get their teaching degrees commuted from Rutland and left their cars during the day in the dusty college parking lot in front of Leavenworth Hall, or in a shady, bowl-like, goldenrod-rimmed lot next to the gym.

The college and the college students didn't much intrude into Jimmy's life. One day, he decided to retire. The school bought his place and he moved away.

Then things changed. The college stripped the building and sided it and turned it into the Public Safety Center. Uniformed school security people sat inside this central location and kept track of illegal parking and nighttime disturbances.

This is how things continued for a long stretch. The campus saw only piecemeal improvements. Over the years, some buildings underwent a few architectural tweaks. A little colonnaded porch, for example, was attached to the front door of Ellis Hall inexpensively improving its looks.

The new nursing building was constructed. The old railroad tracks through the center of campus became the rail trail. The parking lots were enlarged. Blocks of student housing were built in the old bowl-like parking lot below the gym.

This summer, the college campus was transformed. The playing fields were drained and rebuilt, the long-ago boys' soccer field, lush, beautiful, but always wet, was made into a football arena.

A new football stadium now dominates the hill behind the school maintenance building. Parking lots were paved and planted. A big new lot was built in a meadow on the east side of South Street.

Helen Hall died, and her little yellow house, where she'd lived, first with her mother and then alone for half a century, was emptied and rented to an art professor. The college negotiated an option to buy, thinking that down the road Helen's little hillside would make a useful near-stadium parking lot.

Through all of this, Jimmy's house stayed as it was, but sleepy Castleton State College was becoming sleek. Jimmy's house was a throwback, and maybe even, in this new sleek campus context, an eyesore. So, the decision was made to relocate the Campus Security Center across the street. It went up the hill into Elaine Holden's old home, a Carpenter's Gothic place which once was the studio of renowned local painter James Hope.

Jimmy Lynch's little house was stripped of its siding and sat for a while, sad and exposed in its bare-wood and black-tar-paper underwear, until the Castleton Volunteer Fire Department came to burn it down.

Today, two yellow Bob Cats ping and beep and buzz back and forth pushing around broken, blackened timbers and house rubble, some still-bright steel, a scorched hot water tank, boards from the porch. They're filling in the tiny cellar hole, scraping together the earth, which is streaked, light and dark with swaths of charcoal and sand.

Jimmy Lynch's house no longer exists. I admit, for years it seemed a little out of place in the center of the campus, and the college used it well for a long time. Still, it was one of the few reminders of the kind of place CSC once was. I hate to see it gone.

The Hush

Saturday, May 15th, was a day of sun and clouds, temperatures in the low 60s with a little breeze and, early in the morning, the twitter of birds. The CSC parking lots had been cleared, and now they were empty, but would soon be filled, guarded by a crew of public safety employees wearing neon vests.

Across the campus, Suburbans, Toyotas, Dodge trucks and Subarus, were parked up tight around the dorms. These family cars were there to carry home their particular student's year's accumulation of college paraphernalia, blankets and pillows, posters, boom boxes, and, in one case, a little refrigerator heading north to Newport.

Graduation was scheduled for two o'clock , but by eleven parked cars stretched all the way down Castleton's Main Street. Proud, self-conscious families perambulated slowly along campus sidewalks, their daughters wearing flip flops and sundresses much too skimpy for the temperature. Their sons wore sports jackets to which these sons were not accustomed.

The graduation tent had been set up days ago, white, and big enough for Ringling Brothers, topped with an American and a Vermont flag, both unfurling and refurling in the light breeze.

The crowds too had the excited look of Ringling Brothers crowds. Some guests brought their dogs, bull mastiffs, great Danes, lots of labs. Young married alumnae were pushing strollers and holding the hands of tykes wearing tiny green CSC baseball caps. A few red hippy headbands were out there in the crowd, and a girl wearing a sundress and cowboy boots distributed the 223rd Commencement program. Three hundred and fifty students were due to graduate today.

I've seen a lot of these graduations. Year after year I ride up on my bike, park it outside the big tent and watch the opening processional. My parents and my aunts and uncles graduated from Castleton State College, going back to when it was The Normal School, a state teachers' college. I used to host a lunch for these alumnae relatives when they arrived in town at graduation time.

Several of this year's graduates work for us. Some have worked for us since they were freshmen. We're going to lose Kyle LaPine, a senior studio arts major who will leave Castleton to move to Burlington and then plans on living in Montreal, doing his painting and sculpture and tracing his French Canadian family roots.

Courtney Laflamme from Bennington, a drama major who has been in every CSC theater production since her freshman year, will head for Boston. She and her boyfriend want to establish a theater company.

These seem like brave plans in the face of one of the toughest labor markets in recent history, maybe in all history. It's a bleak world that 2010 grads are leaving school to enter. I wonder how these kids will fare.

The CSC music department has become professionally-accomplished over the last few years, and the 27-member wind ensemble playing in a far corner of the big tent opens the day's proceedings with an evocative Celtic sort of melody backed by cymbals and drums.

The academic procession forms up on the steps of Woodruff Hall, a place that looks just as it did in the 1930s at the time of my parents' graduation. The clouds have rolled away. The sky is now blue and sunny. Dogs rest on the lush grass under campus trees. Spectators sit on the stone wall of the Fine Arts Center.

The wind ensemble swings into *Pomp and Circumstance*. The sidewalk down the hill is thronged, lined on both sides with onlookers and undergraduates who, whenever they feel it's appropriate, hoot and cheer.

I push in next to proud, camera-clutching parents and try to get a glimpse, as they come past, of students I know. I look up the hill to Woodruff and see above the pillars on either side of the front door, *Castleton* and above *Castleton* a round oriel window and above the window fluffy clouds and the bright blue sky.

This is a timeless view, and I am watching a timeless rite of passage. I know how it will go—as it goes every year. The tent will fill with the roar of celebrated accomplishment, ovation and applause. It will go on for a long time, but finally the new graduates will spill out, subdued, weary, and say good-bye and get in cars and drive away.

Then the college will be silent, the campus deserted, and a sort of hush will fall over the town. Another year is past, another page turned. At the end of the long, exciting afternoon, there's always this hush.

Ray in Retirement

On April first, after working there ten years, six months, and fourteen days, sixty-six-year-old Ray Ladd retired from Rutland's General Electric Company. He kept track of the time because he couldn't wait to be free and to return home to Castleton.

Now, he says, "I get up in the morning when the sun comes up. It's such a great feeling."

He continues—because this has become a new interest—"I'm paying so much more attention to the birds. I'm watching them more than I ever did. The hummingbirds just came back."

Ray is a man who thrives on small town life. He was born in Benson, but he says Benson is too far away from everything. Castleton, for him, is the place that "can't be beat."

Ray lives on Main Street, with his wife Lois, in a meticulously-kept house behind the Federated Church. Youthful looking, he probably weighs no more than he weighed when he graduated from Fair Haven High school. A past Master of the Lodge, he made a spare and elegant figure, wearing a well-cut suit and Masonic apron, when he walked in the recent Castleton Memorial Day parade.

Ray was one of eight children born to a farm laborer in Benson. The family first lived in a tar paper shack and didn't have a flush toilet until a later move. He remembers sitting at the kitchen table, looking at his hands which he already realized were skillful, and saying, "Ma, I wonder what I'll do when I get older." He knew he wasn't going to follow his father into the fields.

He and all of his siblings graduated from high school. Afterward, Ray went to work at Rutland Plywood. By then he understood that being good with his hands was what was going to allow him to have a life much different than his father's.

Ray Ladd standing in Castleton by the Masonic flagpole. (Pamela Hayes Rehlen photo)

He could visualize something and then easily create it. He moved on to Mal Tool and worked the day shift at this family business, which was located where Rutland's Quick Print is now, for thirty-four years.

When Mal Tool closed, Ray went to G. E. He was a skilled bench machinist, and for that reason it wasn't hard to get a job, but the job was second shift, two- thirty in the afternoon to ten-thirty at night. "I just hated it," he says. "I had no social life. I never saw the grandchildren."

Now, all that's changed. In retirement, Ray is free to be a caretaker of both people and places. "To me, it's almost a duty," he says about the responsibilities he takes on.

Many old timers in Castleton, because of the often hard lives they lived growing up, inescapably developed old time values. Theirs can be a clear vision and a stoic way of seeing the world.

Ray says, "I still think more people should get involved in community things." In winter, he shovels the roof of Dot Burr, a fellow Mason's elderly widow. He does what he can to smooth the path for Betty Zahnlieghter, now in her eighties.

"They trust me," he says matter-of-factly of these two women, and he tries to help them and give them practical advice.

He's been the unofficial caretaker of the Federated Church for years. He knows every inch of this building, and he's been its fierce protector. When tourists visit the graveyard which abuts his house, he goes out and asks if they'd also like a tour of the church next door.

He'll even go up and ring the bells for them. I'll never forget one year waking at midnight to the great pealing of New Year's bells and lying in bed in the Manse listening to Ray across the street, up in the church belfry, joyously ringing in the New Year.

He goes to the Hillside Cemetery on the edge of town and trims the shrubs and paints the maintenance shed. He's one of three overseers of Castleton's fourteen old cemeteries, many long abandoned, grown over, and nearly lost.

Last year, the Historical Society asked him to be a Colonial Day docent at the Higley House. He turned out to be well suited to this. He liked wearing a stove pipe hat and says, "I knew what most of the old stuff was, and how it had been used."

He takes care of the Masonic building's grassy plot in the center of town.

Ray remembers that when he was first married he had three goals. He wanted to be able to buy a chain saw, a bottle of scotch and his own house.

"I've gone beyond that," he laughs. What's become most important is time to spend with his grandchildren, to be with his family, to live in Castleton where he can walk everywhere, and sometimes, for exercise, ride his bike out to the Corners and to Fair Haven.

Now, in retirement, he's able to do exactly what he wants.

The Best Christmas Ever

Quite awhile ago now, we had a Christmas when it seemed nobody was going to be home. My daughters were living far away, and my sister was far away too. No one was going to be able to make it back. However my son was here, and he asked me, a little anxiously, "Will it be much of a Christmas with just us?"

I said, "It might be fine. These things work out. It could be the best one of all."

I don't know why I said that so confidently because I was anxious myself. We seemed unfestively few. My father was still alive then, and I wanted him to have a nice Christmas because he was nearly ninety, and it didn't seem he could have many more. It was going to be just him, my husband, my son and me.

My husband and I went to some town gatherings, and we had our store party, and we went to church. That brought us right up to Christmas day.

In the morning, we made some long distance telephone calls to our other children and my sister. My son came over after picking up his grandfather, who only lived down the street, and we settled in at home going through our usual Christmas rituals.

I have a photo of the four of us on the front room sofa. My son had set his camera's automatic timer and run across the room to join us. There we are all pushed in together in a row. We were laughing. Looking at it now I can't believe that my father was as old as he was. That year, we were all the same age.

I don't remember much about Christmas day. We open gifts one at a time, and when we get hungry we eat breakfast under the tree. I do remember that it was awfully cold, and then it started to snow. It snowed and snowed, but we weren't very aware of it because we were so cozy inside opening those gifts one at a time.

Then it was late afternoon and we had our traditional 'Spirit of Dickens' roast goose dinner. We sat around the table and talked. It grew dark, and my husband said, "Let's get out of the house and go for a drive."

That's when we realized that the snow outside was over a foot deep and the whole town had become silent and dark. The wind pushed the snow around, and it drifted under the street lights. When we'd bundled up and come out into our driveway, it sounded like there was sand or rice blowing in the wind.

The car was warm, and my son and my father got in the back seat. We were headed to Hubbardton. No one else was out. All the houses along Main Street were dark. Perhaps people were tucked in watching television. There was only the blowing snow under the street lights. Town plow trucks had come through once earlier in the day, but now they'd gone home and the snow had deepened dramatically.

When we got up to Hubbardton, we drove the back roads. We slid in spots and slewed around some, but our car was good in snow, and my husband kept going. The cold was intense, the sky clear and black, marked with tiny brilliant stars.

At the top of the long hill on St. John Road, my husband turned off the car lights. I was worried that my father would be alarmed, but when I glanced over my shoulder, I saw he wasn't. He looked happy and excited.

All around us, we saw deep snow and on the distant ridges a few tiny dark farm houses, places he'd known as a boy.

The stars above us were brilliant. It was silent in the car. We went on and on through the deep powdery blowing snow. I wanted that drive to last forever, and now in my memory it does.

Finally we were at the bottom of the hill. My husband turned the lights back on. We headed for Castleton. The stars winked in the terrible cold, but we were warm and comfortable and together, having an adventure.

As I said, that wonderful Christmas we were all the same age.

Hiawatha
at Easter

For the last twenty-five years, I've had a big Easter dinner party at our house to which, in addition to our immediate family, I've invited old friends from town.

I started doing this the second Easter after my mother died. The first Easter, my father came over and went into the front room, and when I walked in to get him for our immediate-family-dinner, I saw that he was crying and I thought, 'I can't have this.'

I couldn't have my father lonely and low at Easter time, so I decided from then on I'd invite more people and make it a party, because I knew my father always came alive when he was interacting with people.

This plan worked perfectly. For many years, we had a table full of old Vermonters and old Castletonians. We had people with whom my father had gone to school and people who lived just down Main Street. For example, we had Frank and Mary—daughter of Hulda Cole—Williamson. We had Florence McCormick, Chris White, Aunt Ruth and Uncle Stan Gibbs.

Rex Hayes at ninety-two. A pensive moment during Easter at The
Manse. (Wenger Rehlen photo)

Even if the weather was bad and spitting snow, we always had a riotous
time, and my father was right in his element. I knew there was no danger of
tears in the front room.

My father's been gone now five years, and the last two years of his life he
wasn't in good enough shape to come up from the Vet's Home, which I always
called the Old Solders' Home, in Bennington to join us. But our pattern of
Easter party-dinners goes on.

A lot of the town oldsters he always enjoyed are also gone, and so things
have changed. This year we had with us, as well as children living away and
local friends, a retired, Cuban, New York City cigar store owner and a Scot far
from the lowland farm on which she'd grown up.

But as I looked around this more cosmopolitan table, I was taken back to an incident many years ago that always rings in my memory like a gentle, ghostly bell.

My father was born in 1911. He went to the Fair Haven Graded School, and he graduated from Castleton Normal School. He was a reader and when he was teaching, he read aloud to his students, particularly in the 1940s and 1950s when school time was filled a lot differently than it is today.

He always read to me, both prose and poetry. One of his favorite poems—how could I not like this too?—was Henry Wadsworth Longfellow's *Hiawatha,* a heroic narrative about Indian life composed in 1855. My father liked the kind of poems you could make fun of, but also be secretly thrilled by.

He loved *Hiawatha* for the same reason he loved Lewis Carroll poems like, *You are Old Father William*. He and I would roar with laughter at the poem's ending, "Be off or I'll kick you downstairs."

Hiawatha starts, "By the shores of Gitche Gumee, By the shining Big Sea-Water." Who could get that sing-song rhyming out of their head? It continues, "Stood the wigwam of Nokomis." I've rolled that line around in my mind pleasurably since the first moment it was read to me.

There was a whole historical, patriotic, inspiring, uplifting, instructional lexicon of poems like these that Castleton Normal School teachers trained in the 1930s were expected to know and read to their Vermont students.

On the long-ago Easter I remember, I had a group of old Vermonter guests hand-selected for my father's enjoyment. I always liked old, and older-than-me, people.

That year, I'd even lured ever-the-loner Margaret Onion to join us. Marg lived on the edge of town on Route 4-A in a beautiful old house. She was roughly my father's age and a fellow teacher. She had a patrician quality, but an unexpected, wry sense of humor.

That's what endeared her to my father. She loved ribald stories and stories that illustrated the foibles of the town 'Old Ones.' I remember her and

Martha Towers telling these stories Sunday mornings out in front of the Federated Church.

What I remembered this Easter was the long ago Easter that my father and I were sitting together at our dining table, and my father started to recite the poem *Hiawatha.*

He began, and then Marg Onion appeared behind him, coming in from the front room, and the two of them, as we all sat and stood around the room, faultlessly recited together, stanza after stanza:

> "By the shore of Gitche Gumee,
> By the shining Big Sea-Water
> Stood the wigwam of Nokomis,
> Daughter of the moon, Nokomis."

I will never forget it.

I regret the passing of a time when the state's educational agenda included—because it was felt to be spirit and life enhancing—the memorization of poetry, when every Vermont student learned poems they loved and were able to recite together seventy years later at an Easter dinner.

A Prospect House Incident

CSC classes are over for another year, and it's time for students to get a summer job. I remember when the best jobs around here were at Lake Bomoseen's three resort hotels. The very best were waitress jobs at the Prospect House. To get in there, you had to be hired by my father.

As head waiter, every spring he'd start receiving applications. He had his legatee girls, the ones who were daughters of the women who had once been waitresses with him when they were all at the Normal School.

Then he had his favorite waitresses. They were farmers' daughters who were going to UVM and majoring in home economics. They could handle anything and were assigned five or six tables a piece. Every summer, they cleaned up financially.

Then, he had me.

I was shy, a compulsive reader who stayed away from people. I was afraid of the fast, loud summertime crowd at the lake.

But when I was eighteen, and about to head off to Castleton State College, it seemed time, and so my father gave me a job. Together, he and I would drive up to the glamorous hotel on Prospect Point.

The lake hotels were ranked, and the Prospect House was seen as the most prestigious, more than the Cedar Grove or the Trak. My father had been head waiter for a number of years at the Cedar Grove working for the formidable owner Mrs. Quinlan, but he'd started at the Prospect House, and when he got a chance to return, he did.

He was a maitre d' out of central casting, whip smart, people savvy, a sharp dresser and movie star handsome.

He told me that he'd first gone up to the hotel when he was in high school. A Fair Haven friend had taken him under his wing, and when they arrived together, my father was immediately hired as a bell hop.

He said that the first day—maybe the first hour—he made more in tips than he would have in a week doing farm work for his father in Benson. He never looked back.

In the 1950s, the Bomoseen resort hotels were right out of backstairs Gosford Park and Downton Abbey. I have no difficulty imagining those worlds, because I've lived in them. There was always so much going on. First, there was a similar swarm of employees who came from Fair Haven and Castleton, and even from far away Rutland.

Jobs were seen as sinecures and handed down in local families. Grounds men took care of the sweeping hotel lawns and the golf course. Men from Fair Haven staffed the boat house. I didn't know any of the chambermaids. I thought of chambermaiding as a lesser job. There was a lot of fiercely-maintained hierarchy in this Downton Abbey-like world.

Young, idealistic and naïve, I didn't have a clue about most of what was going on around me. I just remember some of what I saw. That included the pie ladies, big bosomy local farm wives, who arrived and hurried away to bake in a special room in the back of the cavernous 19th century style kitchen. In the fall, they moved on to make pies at the college.

I remember dishwashers, teen-aged toughs toiling over greasy pots half submerged in streaky, dark, set-tub like sinks. I remember best the cooks, led by head cook Uncle B., southern Blacks who came up for the season and were always a little bored and contemptuous of the locals and the sleepy quality of local life.

My father learned quite soon that I couldn't successfully wait on more than two tables. Eight guests were my limit. He would carefully choose my two tables and make sure they were occupied by patient, kindly, generous tippers, folk who were flattered to have his daughter.

This worked well until he miscalculated and assigned me a new-to-the-hotel *New York Times* editor, his wife and two stylish friends. One night at the beginning of their week's vacation, this foursome stayed much too long at the pre-dinner porch cocktail party.

I'd never in my sheltered life dealt with people who were seriously intoxicated. When the group finally arrived at their table where I was standing at attention, the editor said something unimaginable, never said in Castleton, Vermont at that time to a young woman.

I fled to the kitchen to hide. The cooks, who always knew what was going on everywhere, were up in arms. They grabbed tenderizer mallets and rolling pins and were set to head out to the dining room and take on this depraved interloper.

But, suddenly, my smooth, silver-summer-suited, never-flustered father was there in the kitchen. Always the consummate accommodator, this time was different. Seating assignments were immediately switched. The table was no longer mine.

A top girl—crack UVM home ec. major—was summoned, sent out through those swinging doors and told to give as good as she got. From the set of her jaw, I knew this would be an epic confrontation.

It must have been. Soon after, the editor and his friends were gone.

Every Day
As It Comes

B rian Traverse's grandfather Patrick, a logger from Poultney, came to Castleton when he was working for the Metowee Lumber Company and cutting timber near Birdseye Mountain. The company paid him for his work by giving him land, and he toured the woods at the end of Birdseye Road and marked out for himself a parcel of eighty-seven acres.

Today, Patrick's fifty-two-year-old grandson Brian speaks often of his grandfather. Patrick eventually got out of logging. He bought a two hundred acre farm, known as the Ross Place, just up from his eighty-seven acres, had four children, Robert, George, Shirley, and Sally, and settled down to working the land.

Brian's father was Patrick's son Robert, known as Robbie. In 1949, Robbie married Irene Baker who was part ot a big extended family living in South Wallingford, Tinmouth and Danby.

Following a once-almost-universal custom, the young Traverses lived with his parents for the first years of their married lives. Robbie worked in the woods, but wanted to farm.

In 1960, the couple rented, and then bought, the next door farmhouse with its 250 acres at the juncture of Birdseye Road and old Route 4-A. In this early 1800s house, Robbie and Irene raised twelve children, Sandy, Robert, Martin, Glen, Russell, Sue, Larry 'Skeeter,' Peter, George, Tim, Tom and Brian.

Their mother Irene says proudly that every one of her children graduated from high school. She's also proud that raising twelve children on a Vermont farm in the 1960s and 70s she and her husband managed financially and never needed help from the state. "We never went on welfare."

Eleven of the twelve stayed close by. Only Peter moved away to Virginia.

When the Traverse children grew up, they left for jobs, and a number of them went to work at G. E.

Bob, the oldest son, was still at home, and in 1992 his father gave the family farm to him. But Bob had a hard time. The new Route 4 had gone through making inaccessible some of his good pasture land. He wasn't in a Current Use Program so he was being hit hard for taxes.

He hated the paperwork and the government regulations he faced.

Right at the beginning of hunting season, the state demanded that he take time out to relocate manure piles. That kind of ultimatum was unacceptable to a Traverse. And he was having difficulty getting anyone to pick up the milk from his small dairy herd.

Finally, in frustration, he said he was going to sell the farm and move to Maine. That's when his brother Brian stepped in.

Brian had worked for twenty-six years as a mechanic at the Rutland Country Club, but he'd also always helped out at home. With an inescapable DNA, he wanted to raise cows.

The family arranged that Bob would give the farm back to his father. Then Brian used all his financial resources to clear Bob's back taxes and take over the mortgage. His father then passed the place on to him.

Brian's wife Kathy was dead set against it. "You're going to die trying to keep the farm." But he's had it now more than ten years.

To keep things going, Brian drives milk truck long distance for the Robies in Orwell, and Kathy is a hair dresser at Special Effects Salon in Castleton.

Brian's brother Bob milks for him twice a day. The Traverses once had a big barn, but it burned in 1973. They've replaced it with a free stall arrangement and a six cow California flat parlor.

Brian says, "Our cows never see the barn, only when they're milked. They're fed outside in a ring feeder. We do everything the simplest way."

The farmhouse has the serene, but battered, coziness of the oldest farm homesteads. This is where Irene Traverse, now eighty, lives. She says she's seldom alone. That's probably because to say that the Traverses are clannish and land-connected would be a colossal understatement.

Irene has a wall of school photos of her thirty-six grandchildren, twenty-three great-grandchildren, and one Woodbury, who is an honorary Traverse.

Brian remembers when thirty-six of his relatives lived along this dirt road. Every morning, school bus driver Rose Baptie would pick up what was known as the Birdseye Gang.

It doesn't seem that a lot has changed. On an unseasonably hot April day, brother Bob, who now lives up on his Uncle George's original farmstead, is driving the cows in from pasture. Brother Larry is at the barn; brother Tom drives past and waves.

The Traverses sell raw milk, grass-fed beef, and eggs. Brian says they're looking for a local cheese maker to whom they can sell their milk. Brian says, "I want to work all day right here, not off the farm."

A lot of people don't realize that the Traverses are still milking. "But we are," he says.

He and his mother, who seem close and comfortable together, sit at the kitchen table and say "We just take every day as it comes."

Brian Traverse on the farm. (Pamela Hayes Rehlen photo)

Hayden's
Pussy Willows

F or a number of years, every spring, right before Easter, an armload
of pussy willows would appear at my back door. The first year, I was
puzzled, but I took them in and stood them up in a big vase in our front
room, and every one who came for our annual Easter dinner admired them.

I soon learned that they were from Hayden Hughes, a watchmaker who
lived way out on the edge of Castleton on Belgo Road. I sent him a Thank You
note, and the next year when they appeared, I sent him a Thank You note,
and then I got a phone call.

Hayden said, "Stop sending me those Thank You notes. They're not necessary. You're one of my Pussy Willow Ladies, and every spring I will always
bring you a bunch of pussy willows."

Hayden seldom came into town. He lived a pretty solitary life, although he
had a wife and two children of whom he was intensely proud. I almost never
ran into him, and several springs ago, there were no pussy willows by the
back door. I learned that he had cancer, and then very shortly after, I read his

obituary in the paper. I missed the rite-of-spring pussy willows, and I was sad to think that Hayden was gone.

He was a true eccentric. He and his family moved to Castleton from Poultney. He flew the red and yellow Pendragon flag. This is the kind of thing the most romantic Poultney Welsh do. As a watchmaker, a solitary craftsman, he had a route and picked up repairs from area businesses including Ellis Jewelers in Fair Haven and Freeman's in Rutland. He took watches home to labor over in his basement workroom.

Out in back of his house, he had a threatening wolf-hybrid dog, and he always came to his door with a gun tucked into his waistband.

He had a sometimes disconcertingly-Rabelaisian sense of humor, but he was proud of the fact that his son Tom loved history as much as he did and was employed at a historic site in New York State

Every Sunday for years, Bill Hart, unofficial town mayor, and Hayden, like naughty school boys sat up in the back of the Federated Church, close to the choir loft, critiquing the week's sermon. Marg Onion also sat up in back. Marg was a school teacher, a Smith graduate, (another of the pussy willow recipients) a fellow history buff, and a classy lady much admired by Hayden. She would tell the two of them, the "Amen boys," to keep it down.

I first got to know Hayden when I called him to see if he would fix the wind-up clock that had sat on top of my Fair Haven grandmother's china cabinet all my growing-up years.

I also brought him my father's, grandfather's, and great-great grandfather's pocket watches. My father wanted the best one of these to be handed on to my son. Hayden said that all the old farmers had these kinds of pocket watches. He'd seen hundreds of them.

I remember when my husband roped Hayden into trying to fix the town clock. The clock, in the cupola of the library, hadn't worked for decades. My husband has Swiss-German jeweler and watchmaker ancestors, he's good at fixing almost anything, and so he told Hayden that the two of them could probably do it together.

Bill Mulhollnad, fire chief at the time, brought over the hook and ladder truck and extended the ladder right up to the clock face. My children scampered around and called up to Daddy and Mr. Hughes who were laboring in a little dirty library attic space.

The two of them managed to reaffix the hands to the face of the clock. But the bushings needed to be replaced, and Hayden was a watchmaker, not a clock repairer, and my husband was just a confident amateur, so they only managed to fix it temporarily.

Later, my husband got Alan Grace, 'The Clock Doctor,' from Middletown Springs, to come up and do the job right.

This last Thursday night, I was away at choir in Rutland and got home late. I came into our kitchen, and on my grandmother's round table in the center of the room was a great armload of pussy willows.

I was dumbfounded. My husband said, "Hayden's son Tom was here. He's gotten a new job working for the Chimney Point Historical Site. He's moved back to Vermont, and he's now living in Middlebury. He got the list of his father's pussy willow ladies from his mother, and he went out and cut the pussy willows and he went around and delivered them all today."

My husband said, "Tom looks exactly like his father. When he carried the pussy willows in, I thought it was Hayden standing here in the kitchen."

The Bunkhouse

Our family cottage on Lake Bomoseen is an Adirondack-style building surrounded by oaks and hemlocks. It was built in the 1880s for a Rutland minister who came out here to Castleton to write sermons in the shadow of the rocky mountain that rises abruptly behind us.

After the tenure of the minister and his descendants, some other people bought this west shore place and tried to clear the land and get in more sun, but they were never really satisfied with the results, and so they sold to us, a young couple, at the time too occupied with the demands of small children to notice afternoon shadows.

The property has been steadily growing back for the more than twenty-five years we've owned it. From our screened-in front porch, now surrounded by hemlocks, we no longer have a clear view of the lake, but if we walk down a wooded path, we get to our dock and a circular platform we've built at the end of the dock which extends a good way out into the lake.

Sitting here, we are able to see all up and down a vast expanse of water surface. It's like leaving a coat closet to walk out onto the prairie.

A lot has happened over the years in this cottage, and it occurs to me that a good part of it has gotten away from me. This was the "time out" place. That's why I didn't realize that, even here, time was marching on.

Our cottage set up is really two cottages: the not very big 'big house' and the bunkhouse. The minister who created all of this wanted a study for his sermon writing, and so he constructed a little building forty feet from the main house. When we first came out to spend our summer here, we had a small child, a toddler and a baby. They gravitated toward the sermon writing study immediately.

This little building was a mess. The former owners had used it to store rakes, tools, bags of charcoal, their grill, and finally, a lot of broken junk which no one wanted to use precious summer time to take to the dump. It was gratifying to set it all to rights, and when we finished, it occurred to us that this would be our children's place. At first, they had some concern about sleeping alone away from us where large spiders had been spotted during the cleaning out process, but they moved beyond this apprehension and with all their favorite possessions from town set about creating a play house sort of summer home.

There came to be four children in the bunkhouse. The spiders had met their match. We'd had one more baby, who slept for a time in the doll's crib; then we had bunk beds built. Terrible fights broke out, but there were also stretches of quiet reading, and an added-to-every-year row of paperbacks grew long on a beam behind the top bunk.

We'd provided two bureaus. How could I have imagined they would be cheerfully shared? I often came upon someone's entire summer wardrobe dumped out on the floor. The only chair was a Naugahyde beanbag, which belonged to my son and in which he was never prepared to allow any of his sisters to sit. A stock of curios, little ceramic horses made in Taiwan and prizes won at last year's Rutland Fair were arranged along the sills of the three bunkhouse windows.

Our cottage has an outhouse and water pumped up from the lake through a hose like a giant black snake. The bunkhouse has a little sink in the corner. This was always seen by the children as a glamorous adult amenity which allowed them to maintain their independence, and when it was time to brush their teeth before bed not have to come over to where we were.

In our family, soda and candy were forbidden so empty soda cans and candy wrappers were hidden under the bunkhouse floor. (This trove only recently came to light.) On the bunkhouse front porch, four small Adirondack chairs, just like the adults' next door, sat scorned. What did we take them for? Finally, my husband and I went over and got the little chairs and carried them to the big house to use ourselves as footstools or to offer to very young children who came to visit.

The babies became toddlers, and then little people who swam all day and fought with tremendous ferocity at night. Muffled cries and the sounds of crashes as territorial prerogatives were made clear reached us at one or two in the morning. My husband would have to get up and bring a kicking, shouting child back to the terrible humiliation of a night sleeping on a cot close to his parents.

A lot was going on in the bunkhouse, most of which we knew nothing about. We were easily circumvented because I read all the time, and my husband drove into town to do his work.

During the long afternoons, I sat on our screened-in porch, and when I put my book down, I heard the ripple and splash of the close by lake. I sometimes imagined that I was on a boat with a gentle wash across my bow. However, my boat was tied up securely at a noisy dock. The bunkhouse crashes or screams were like the sound of uncouth stevedores loading me for a sailing to unknown lands.

The little people were getting to stand as tall as my shoulder and then my ear. They no longer wanted to swim all day long. Some of the fights, now that everyone was big and strong, became truly alarming, and the fights never stopped. Bunkhouse living for four was now untenable, but we had no more space.

The 'big house' contains only a kitchen, a livingroom, and one bedroom. Inspired by our visit to a Girl Scout camp, my husband ordered a state-of-the-art tent and tent platform, and we set this up for two summers.

That tent—in every respect—was a dark place. The twenty-foot-square platform was erected in the gloomy back of our property. The tent was made of a heavy, funereal, canvas that zipped closed tight at the ends. Although I was predisposed to admire it because the canvas creation was elegantly Edwardian—like something Byrd had taken with him to the south Pole, I couldn't get away from the fact that once the end flaps were zippered shut, not a ray of light came in. It was frightening, the pitch-blackness that had to be entered, usually as one was thinking how large spiders continued to be a feature of life at our cottage.

Also, for one of the two daughters we moved in here, this was a period of early adolescent slovenliness and a wildish friend of whom we didn't approve. At the end of the season, when the tent was finally taken down and the contents came to light, there were drifts of smelly clothing, copies of the teen magazine YM, techno cassettes, and way in one corner, behind the chest of drawers, an empty bottle of Old Mr. Boston.

That tent is now stored somewhere in our barn back in town, and the tent platforms only continuing function is to serve as the bar for our annual Fourth of July parties.

After the canvas was taken away, I'd go out sometimes and stand on the wooden flooring. All around me were big splashes of melancholy sunlight because our beech trees are suffering some kind of blight and no longer fully leaf out. I'd look across the scruffy lawn between the cottage and the bunkhouse, where, once the dog days of summer have begun, the soil is too thin and poor to support green grass, and where the children exacerbated the problem by once setting up a volley ball court.

The next summer our oldest daughter got a job, which finished at eleven. My husband and I were asleep by eleven, the bunkhouse and tent silent (possibly misleadingly so.) Sometimes, I woke and lay in bed listening to little night sounds, the heavy-bodied snuffle of a raccoon out hunting, the brushing and twig snapping of a deer grazing close by.

Down at our dock, I heard the lap and gurgle of the lake. It came to me with a sense of foreboding that the boat I sometimes imagined I was occupying had grown quiet because there was now so much more on board. Then I'd hear my daughter's ride, the faint approach of a car coming down through the woods, the whispery crunch of tires over loose gravel. This was my oldest child's last summer at the lake.

The next year, with his sisters moved to the tent and town, the bunkhouse became the exclusive domain of my son, the feisty little character who as a toddler had managed to fall out of our upstairs window flat onto his back, missing by inches an Adirondack chair which would have pierced him through. He'd been in our bedroom fighting so he felt that it wouldn't be wise to attract attention. We came upon him as he got to his feet, dazed, but unhurt and staggered off toward the bunkhouse like a resolute midget drunk.

Lying on his top bunk the summer before college, rap blasting from state-of-the-art stereo equipment, he had far different concerns. When he wanted company, he let in our youngest daughter, who envied him his Reservoir Dogs movie poster, his stereo equipment, his neon tubing beer signs, and most of all, because she was still sharing the funereal tent, his own little building.

When my son was no longer at the cottage, I, too, stayed in town. (I should say that these places are only six miles apart.) My husband carried on as usual. He was lonely out at the lake without me. "Should we just sell?" he asked, exasperated because, as the weeks went by, it became apparent to both of us that I wasn't going to come out even for a swim.

▲▲▲

This year, something was different. In June, I got in the car, and I drove out to the cottage. I noticed things. I saw that the young beeches and ashes, the oaks and hemlocks, have been coming on steadily. Trees are growing where—

long ago—our son fell onto bare ground. From something bright and raw, the atmosphere has gently darkened. Time, here, has passed.

I went into the 'big house,' which has the sweet wood smell of old hay lofts, and I climbed upstairs and looked at our bed. The summer before, my husband had pulled it out into the center of the room so that he would have an early morning view of the sun rising over the lake. Had I been there, I would never have gone along with such an unorthodox furniture arrangement, but, now, I realized it had its charm, and I left it where it was.

I walked over to the bunkhouse. Part of our raft was being stored in here. I saw window boxes filled with the powdery corpses of last summer's flowers. The torn Reservoir Dogs movie poster lay on the floor. The little sink was spattered with mouse droppings. Far back in the gloom, stripped to its ticking, one bunk bed mattress remained. I saw that the bunkhouse was as much an abandoned storage shed as it had been the day we first arrived.

▲▲▲

Two weeks later, my husband, our youngest daughter, and I drove out to the cottage with a car full of household basics. I made up a bed in the big house for my daughter, but the next day she told me that this arrangement wasn't satisfactory. She gathered up an armload of cleaning supplies, and she headed to the bunkhouse saying, "If I have to be stuck out here, at least it's going to be comfortable."

She called her brother, and he arrived with the summer loan of a truck full of his college dorm furniture. The two of them went to work, and I watched a bunkhouse-bound imitation oriental rug, a sofa, an odd color leather chair and matching ottoman, glass shelving, an arc lamp, Venetian blinds, new movie posters, plants, pillows, armloads of books, clothing, toiletries. Over in the big house, I wandered around. As always, I read. My usual melancholia seemed inappropriate with this close by tornado of rehabilitative activity.

Finally, my son drove off in an empty truck. I made supper for my daughter, my husband and me. We had fresh corn and grilled chicken. A little breeze sprang up on the lake bringing us the smell of dark water, mingling with our dinner table scents of candlewax and phlox. On our radio there was gentle music and little surfs of applause, a live broadcast from Tanglewood. We were settling in.

A few nights later, my husband and daughter decided to take an evening bike ride. I was staying behind and wanted to read. My daughter took me over to the bunkhouse and told me I'd be most comfortable in her leather chair. She settled me here and went off with her father. "Don't touch anything," she said, "or you never get in here again." (The bunkhouse door was always locked and the key hidden.)

I sat in my children's comfortable chair. The bunkhouse was transformed by the dark, richly-scrolled, rug, the sofa, reading lights, books, plants, good music from hidden speakers, environment-conscious toiletries rimming the (now immaculate) little sink.

In all our summers, my husband and I had never lived with this level of creature comfort. I kept putting down my book and looking around. I couldn't think of anything I had to do here, and so I just sat peacefully in this reborn room that was no longer mine.

The wind rose, warm gusts gently buffeting the bunkhouse, and out on the porch, I heard the first gentle spatterings of rain. I knew, now, there was no question that I was in a boat, and I had left the dock. I was already a little distance from the shore, and I was steadily moving away, with the scent-filled summer wind behind me, blowing against my sails.

Castleton
Quarry Holes

Quarry holes are everywhere around Castleton. This is slate country. Quarrying, really strip mining, is one of Vermont's old, heavy industries, like all rock extraction and like lumbering. It's hard on the land, but it has a long, proud history. It has employed generations of Vermonters and produced tons of useful product. In the search for new sources of slate, test blasts are carried out, and quarry holes are left behind. Now, after more than a hundred and fifty years of exploration, hidden quarry holes are everywhere .

They are places of great power.

Certain features all quarry holes have in common. One is that they are a little scary. It's hard not to speculate on what could live in the depths of a typical, stagnant water, middle of the woods, marked with drowned, rotting logs, quarry hole. Nothing that anyone would want to meet when, for example, swimming in them.

That's what I wanted quarry holes to be when I was growing up, nature's swimming pools. I thought it would be wonderful to be able to go into the woods and come to a hidden glade and have my own private place to swim. But quarry holes aren't like that.

I kept visiting a quarry hole in the woods behind the Pencil Mill school house where my family lived, and I was so filled with unease I felt breathless. I never could make myself enter that water. The atmosphere was too ominous.

Quarry holes deep in the woods are silent. They seem to gather silence around them. They are hushed and still and green, places of gently decaying plant life. Big trees, often pines, fall into their black depths. It's always black depths with quarry holes, and it's never possible to see very far down. Because the water's stagnant, it's full of algae and the fallen tree trunks are drowned in darkness.

On a September day my son took me to a quarry hole I'd never visited before. We drove to Green Dump, the boat access on the west side of Lake Bomoseen. It was mid-week and school was back in session so the parking lot held only a Dodge Ram and a Chevy, both hooked up to boat trailers. It was a day for old men to be out by themselves fishing and dreaming.

A single outboard buzzed full throttle down the middle of the quiet lake. My son and I climbed to the top of the Green Dump parking tiers, entered a tattered woods, followed a twisting, slatey path, and up ahead we saw a cliff face and a quarry hole which struck me as looking like a tiny Yosemite.

Except for an occasional crow caw, it was as silent here as these places always are. This was an old, two-part excavation, the surface of the water shining black, and birches growing out of the slate outcroppings around the water's edge. The piled up slate slag had grown over with white pine, hemlock and beech. Mustard yellow leaves were bright above the quarry hole's black water.

Half of the quarry excavation was a dark, autumnal tarn, deeply shadowed. Little fish flicked in its green algae depths. The other half of the quarry hole was sunny and surrounded by pulverized slate and great slate slabs, blasted out and left, probably a hundred years earlier.

The author at the quarry hole. (Wenger Rehlen photo)

A rock face rose on the west, a dark wall of stone, topped by stunted woods. Feeling more peaceful than I had in a long time, I sat in the sun, next to a weathered rope hanging down from a pine and clearly used once, probably by intrepid boys, to swing out over the water. Far, far overhead a jet left a plumy white trail across the pale sky.

Like every quarry hole, it was a site of failure and abandonment, a wounded spot, but so eerily still and filled with mystery, it seemed a holy place.

Fair Haven Boy

I always intended to write an article about my born- in-1911, raised in West Haven/Fair Haven father. I was going to interview my father. I was going to title the piece Fair Haven Boy.

I would have included my father's standing on the Adams Street bridge (peaceful Indian Summer day, golden late afternoon sun, the Poultney River moving swiftly below) and realizing that he'd stood on this same Fair Haven bridge—a bridge which didn't look much different than it had in 1921—eighty years earlier and faced a gang of tough South Side boys. That long-ago day he didn't know if he had a future, and now he stood on the same spot, amazed to be able to look back to such a distant time.

When Charles Laramie, one of my father's closest boyhood friends, died, my father and I went to the Fair Haven funeral, a mammoth memorial event held at St. Mary's Catholic Church.

My father told me afterward that instead of concentrating on the gleaming casket down in front of this high-vaulted serene space, he was remembering being in here chasing John Durick. The two five-year-old boys were playing Cowboys and Indians and Durick invoked the concept of church sanctuary and dashed into Saint Mary's to be safe.

But my father was a Protestant. He didn't subscribe to the concept of 'church sanctuary.' He pursued little John Durick right down St. Mary's long shining center aisle and thrashed him at the alter.

Ten years ago when passenger service was resumed from New York City to Rutland, Vermont, Fair Haven once again became a train stop. My father and I drove out to the dilapidated Fair Haven depot and sat in my car for awhile, my father telling me that at the end of the First World War, with the rest of the townspeople, he remembered being here at this then smartly-maintained building everyone waiting for returning troops, everyone waving bright little American flags.

In the dead of winter when in the business center of Fair Haven the snow was deep, and deep on the hill which led down toward the Lyons shirt factory, my father as a young boy would hitch his sled to the back of passing cars. It was dangerous to get rides this way, but all the town boys did it. One of my father's friends was killed hitching a ride from a motorist who had no idea he was pulling a boy on a sled. Random, terrible deaths were part of 1920's Vermont small town life.

 Relying on my father's total recall and the fact that he knew everyone in Fair Haven, I intended to recount these sorts of incidents. My father remembered who townspeoples' parents were, where people were born, where they now lived; he maintained a vast personal data bank. My father had an ability to suggest the larger significance of small town events and small town people's personalities. He never developed his material, but continually gathered material that was crying out to be developed. I guess I'd label his forte inchoate philosophical reminiscence.

My piece got away from me, because I never wanted to sit down and start the interview process when both my father and I knew it was the signal that I imagined he wasn't going to be around much longer.

And I didn't understand, then, how old age slips into really old age and, finally, into shadows, dark sad places once beyond my imagining.

But I've decided to take up Fair Haven Boy again.

My father's still with me. He has prostate cancer—but for any man over ninety that's pretty common. His walk has become tottery because of early Parkinson's Disease. He's extremely deaf which makes spontaneous social interaction, once his forte, impossible.

People who know my father and who appear in front of him suddenly, briefly, when he and I are on the street or in the doctor's office are unsure whether he realizes who they are. Almost always, he does. As we drive home, after I fill him in on whom we just saw, he tells me all about them, where they lived, who their parents were.

My father's kept his marbles. He's kept his sense of humor, his cynicism, his irony, all the difficult parts of his personality, but he's also managed to hold onto his charm and his social orientation.

Our RSVP Bonebuilders exercise group, of which my father is the oldest member, meets in the front parlor of the Fair Haven Congregational Church. My father remembers coming here for Sunday School. He remembers his Sunday School teachers, laconic Fair Havenites speaking to him with the cultural expectations of long, long ago.

Next door to the church is the former high school from which he graduated in 1930. He should have graduated in 1929, but he flunked Latin because he had a morning job delivering telegrams and was never able to make the class. My father said that at that time it wasn't unusual to repeat a high school senior year, even an eighth grade year, if you weren't sure what you were going to do with your life and wanted more opportunity to think about it.

The grade school my father attended is a few mighty stone throws distant from the old Fair Haven High School and the Congregational Church. Over on Dutton Avenue is my grandmother's house purchased in the 1930s when my father was a student at the Normal. Later, when my father was teaching in Forrest Dale, Brownsville, and West Windsor, before he got married,

11 Dutton Avenue was just a place to pick up mail.

Now, with two giant silver maples out in the front yard, my father has a 1,100 square foot house in Castleton, snug, all-on-one-floor, facing south so that the sun floods in through a living room picture window.

Before his growing deafness made it impossible, he sat with a black plastic Sony AM/FM radio balanced on a tiny footstool and listened to the news. I'd find him in the morning in his sun-filled, silver maple-shaded house sitting bare foot and snug at the kitchen table eating his bowl of Cheerios, reading the morning paper.

Now, I bring the paper each morning when I visit Haven Health and try to coax him into looking at it. I test him. We get out his reading glasses, and I say, "Can you read that?" He reads it out clear and strong, London bombings, a hurricane approaching. "Do you care about this?" I ask. He doesn't. The paper drops to his lap.

The Fair Haven Boy now has a feeding tube. That's why he's here in the rehab unit of Haven Health Nursing Home, which was once the Rutland Hospital. He's building up enough strength to go home, and he's watching the other residents, almost all of them younger than he is.

Many of these residents are in wheel chairs. They have diabetes and have lost a leg. Determined old people are inching their way past where my father sits, in a premium front hall seat. The old people are using walkers with front legs on wheels, back legs ending in bright yellow tennis balls.

I've learned that there is a whole alternate universe inhabited by the elderly, starting right at the edge of the busy vigorous world of those who can easily see and hear and walk. When my father and I go to urologist Dr. Ernie Bove's to have the quarterly shot necessary to keep prostate cancer at bay, Dr. Bove's waiting room is filled with the variously incapacitated elderly.

Old people covertly study each other. They compare their physical conditions. The elderly in Dr. Bove's waiting room seem like children on a kindergarten playground, shy but eager to make new friends. I see my father looking approvingly at the well-spoken old gent across the room wearing a

*Rex Hayes as a teenager standing in downtown Fair Haven, Vermont.
(Hayes family collection)*

flat cap. My father's generation all wore flat caps. No Fair Haven man went around bare headed.

Everyone visiting Dr. Bove's has with them a caregiver, a spry younger wife, a nursing home employee, a son or daughter. Helping my father into the car, I've never felt more a part of the human family or a part of the poignant inescapable human condition.

My grandmother was admitted into Sager's Nursing home by my aunt who lived in Barre with a husband who had Alzheimer's. My aunt couldn't both care for her husband and keep driving down to take care of her mother. In Fair Haven, Sagers was the rough equivalent of the Poor Farm, in that the Fair Haven old faced it with dread. But they understood that old people were to cause their families no trouble. The elderly were to go to Sagers to be warehoused until they died.

Haven Health isn't like that. There's a lot of life in here, but my father isn't responding. Maybe he's locked in a Sager's mindset. He hasn't been sent here to die, but his stories have dried up. All he wants to tell me is that he's been left too long sitting out in the hall.

"You can get up and move around," I tell him.

He has to walk a fine line, not acting out (he acted out when he first arrived from the hospital and still had hospital drugs in his system) and not being passive. All of my father's stories have dried up except that he tells me about visiting my mother here, in this hospital, when my sister was born. (My birth was during the war years. No visit was possible.)

He tells me he came up to see my mother on the fifth floor, but I'm not sure the old Rutland Hospital had a fifth floor. From our seat today out on Haven Health's front porch glider, I scan brick walls trying to gauge under the thick camouflage of ivy how many floors this old building has.

It makes me think of The Human Fly's visit to Fair Haven, a story I always intended to include in my father's Fair Haven Boy reminiscences. In the 1920s a wily character rolled into Fair Haven and took bets that he wouldn't be able to go up the side of the center-of-town Hotel Allen in the manner of a human fly.

Fair Havenites of the 1920s were not a credulous lot (nor are they today.) The Human Fly proposed to crawl straight up the hotel's front wall, six floors if you included the basement and northeast corner turret, to the roof. Bets that he couldn't do it were confidently made by townspeople, people who considered themselves to be good judges of what in this world was possible and not possible.

An enormous, excited, anticipatory crowd gathered. But, somehow, it had never been stipulated exactly how the Human Fly was to reach the roof— that is if there were any means he couldn't use—and so when the time came, he went up not a featureless section of hotel wall, but by using the building's window sills and decorative ledges.

Today, when I look at an old photo of the hotel, I think that even this was quite a feat, but the 1920's crowd was outraged. They felt that they'd been suckered, and the Human Fly was lucky to get out of town alive. My father enjoys this story. But I never heard it when I was growing up. He told it to me for the first time about eight years ago.

A Fair Haven story, a favorite of his, that my father's told me all of my life is one I've never liked much, maybe because the characters seemed crude and the situation threatening.

It must have taken place around 1900 and immediately became part of Fair Haven folklore. It was the account of teenaged Cassias Crandell and Mr. Howard. I imagine Mr. Howard as a Wild Bill Bonhomme, the Northeast Kingdom outlaw/psychopath created by the writer David Mosher in his novel *Disappearances*.

Mr. Howard lived up in the marsh, which is the swampy area near Inman Pond, Fair Haven's reservoir. (I add parenthetically that no reservoir in the state could look less like a body of water serving a municipal function than rattlesnake infested Inman Pond.)

The Howards, according to my father, were a rough lot living in isolated cabins. My father didn't know how they supported themselves exactly, maybe by trapping.

Cassias Crandell was visiting up in Howard country. It was early spring and lunchtime. Mr. Howard decided that refreshment was called for and made Cassias a minnow sandwich.

"Eat it, Cassias," he commanded. (He had a shotgun.)

"I don't want to Mr. Howard."

"Eat it Cassias."

That's what I've said often to my father in his extreme old age. I used to say that when he claimed to have no appetite, when he told me he didn't have the strength to get dressed and go to Bonebuilders, when he said that he couldn't walk any farther. As a true Fair Haven Boy, it always rallied him. It got us through some tough patches.

"Eat it Cassias."

Rex Hayes in his early eighties standing in front of his one-time Fair Haven High School. (Hayes family collection)

Visiting My Father at The Old Soldiers' Home

Outside the front door of the Bennington Veterans' Home, for years known as the Old Soldiers' Home, there's a roofed cement deck where rain or shine, temperatures sweltering or plummeting, the vets sit and smoke. The whole front of the building smells faintly of the sweet, sharp aroma of cigarettes, a smell that brings back the 1950s when every public place smelled like this.

The vets sit in wheel chairs, or motorized chairs. Presently there are about 165 in residence. The home can take up to 180. Some veterans have lost a leg. Most wear white elastic, knee high stockings with bright orange name tags. They sport services insignia mesh caps: USS Washington, Navy, United States Marines.

Coming up the entrance ramp with a basket of the laundry that I take home each week, I am often overcome with nostalgia and a sense of loss. I remember a world where everyone had a package of Chesterfields. In that world my father was strong and healthy, clear thinking and able to take care of himself.

When I was a little girl, he drove my mother, my sister and me in our 1956 Ford past the Bennington Vets' Home, and he told us to watch for the deer. That was so typical of entertainment in 1950s Vermont, craning out the car window to catch a glimpse of the deer at the Bennington Old Soldiers' Home.

On a glorious day (and there have been many in the two years since my father has come down here to live) the approximately eighty-seven acre park land that surrounds the Vets' Home looks grand.

Bright grassy fields stretch between Route 7 and Mt. Anthony High School. The Deer Park, the Deer Park picnic area, and two gazebos lie to the north of a long, flag-lined entrance drive. Down the drive and across busy, busy Route 7 are a number of eateries: Jensens, the Blue Ben Diner and a Tastee Freez snack bar.

Around behind the many flat roofed, brick, one story wings added in the 1970s to the original house—which was built as a summer retreat by Seth B. Hunt a successful New York businessman in 1860—are additional parking lots, well-maintained barns, and the soldiers' cemetery, headstones perfectly aligned in long rows, neat little crochet wicket shapes in marble.

After a visitor has signed in at the front desk, North-Wing runs to the left. Once through the swinging doors this wing has a benign, reassuring medicinal smell, like a 1950's drugstore.

Looking into North Wing rooms is like looking into snug caves, little bulwarks that have been thrown up against life's battering forces. The morning sun falls across beds with afghans from home, across pillows and televisions, walls with crucifixes and pictures of long ago weddings, of grandchildren, of puppies and kittens, soft comforting images.

These rooms proclaim safety and normalcy. The men who live here are 'pretty good.' They travel around in motorized wheel chairs or use walkers. They look out into the hall, which is brighter than their snug rooms, to see who's passing. They converge in their motorized equipment at the nurses' station where they watch a big bright television or play games or have the paper read to them.

They speak up and loudly voice complaints.

A wiry little guy, desperation evident, shouts, "Jesus Christ, I know how to do this. Leave me alone."

He's struggling, but he's OK because a young nurses' aid patiently stands close by, holding both his walker and the chair into which he's trying to lower himself.

Sometimes the hallways at the Vets' Home seem like undersea corridors with fish of different size and temperament swimming slowly past. It's like the movie 'Finding Nemo.' Big fish cruise by majestically, large dreamy men who seem to be in good shape except for their dependence on motorized wheel chairs, smaller darting fish, perpetually agitated men shoving along their walkers. A lone busy fish, a brusque energetic old guy, who stomps around delivering the mail, schools of placid, well-behaved men-fish (a few women are here too) being pushed by aids, and some always-by-themselves men, like unique sea creatures, octopuses perhaps, who are able to walk unaided but with huge, alarming, spastic gaits.

Sunlight finds its way into, and across the linoleum floors, of all the wings of these flat roofed, 1970's era, one-story buildings. Outside, the Bennington Garden Club has planted banks of phlox, cosmos, black-eyed daises, and hollyhocks.

Surrounded by drifts of flowers, some vets sit out in the A-Wing gazebo and smoke. On a beautiful summer's day, among the hollyhocks and delphinium, they look like guests at a surreal Alice in Wonderland tea party.

A room near the A-Wing nurses' station is roofed and sided with glass and filled with the garden club's specimen houseplants. In here the sun is dazzlingly intense. Picture puzzles are stacked against the wall. A phone rings continually. A fine-featured, beret-wearing old man—it's easy to imagine that he might have been a member of the French resistance and is here as an honorary American War Veteran—wears headphones and dozes all day in a wheeled bed close to a giant Christmas cactus.

Like Conastoga wagons, wheel chairs circle the nurses' station, multiplying dramatically as mealtimes approach.

"Sunderland is a nice town." A grizzled vet, killing time before he can get in to eat, has pulled up to one of the nurses.

Pushing the medicine trolley among the vets as if it were a Good Humor cart, the nurse replies over her shoulder, "Land up there was cheap."

"At one time," the old fellow corrects her, wheeling away triumphant, "but land ain't cheap there no more."

Vets have to assert themselves every once in a while. Every once in a while, vets have to push back.

▲▲▲

One of the reasons I chose the Vets' Home in Bennington for my father is the atmosphere. The place doesn't feel bleak or despairing. It feels like a bustling military infirmary. Many of these old guys are in terrible shape, but it seems as if they're suffering horrendous war wounds.

A lot of the doors along the hall have framed photographs of the men who now live in these rooms as they looked during their military service. Handsome young men full of life in Second World War army and navy uniforms. My father has his photograph showing him, flaxen-haired, weighing probably 140 pounds, standing in front of a tent at Fort Devens.

Every Tuesday, when my sister and I drive down to visit, I push my father all around the building and often all around outside. He rides in his "little cart." Advancing Parkinson's has made it difficult for him to think of the correct words for things, and he's fallen back on using orotund equivalents. He has mixed feelings about being confined to a wheel chair and so that is now referred to—with slight contempt—as a "little cart."

We head off over the bright linoleum. We go down the length of A-Wing, past the caged, long haired guinea pig who looks like a little skunk and who doesn't get much time from anyone. Along the backstretch of North Wing, we gain on a number of slowly moving motorized wheel chairs sporting day glo pennants. We pass the kitchen and look in.

Rex Hayes in his thirties, a weatherman during World War Two.
This is a photo he sent home to the author, 'Baby Pam'. (Hayes family
collection)

My father was a teacher and a school principal, but in the summers, for a good part of his life, he was the headwaiter at the Prospect House Hotel on Lake Bomoseen. He knows kitchen scenes like this one.

Next, we head into the activity room filled with sun, crafts projects, newspapers, a caged bird, computer terminals—which don't interest my father.

Out into the hall, we circle a pool table, hurry away from the doorway to the Alzeimers wing—which can seem like the path to the Eye of Modor.

Then we go up the shining linoleum to the laundry room, like the kitchen, a center of activity to which my father can relate. We head down a quiet hall to the bland non-denominational chapel, the non-denominational aspect so vigorously maintained that the place offers little comfort. No one's ever in here. This is where the two of us, me sitting in a back pew, have a weekly talk.

My father sighs, a huge sigh, "I never expected to live this long." Then he yawns, an uncontrollable Parkinson's yawn.

"What's going on in Fair Haven?" He asks. He misses Fair Haven, where he grew up.

Some weekends I get a phone call. My father is thinking clearly during the week, and when my sister and I visit. I only get these confused phone calls on the weekends.

When he reaches me at home, facilitating Nurse John says, "Your father is on the phone. He wants to speak to you."

But I know that my father can't hear me very well over the phone. Still, I accept the call, and the little plaintive voice begins, "Can you come pick me up? I'm down at the train station."

He means the Castleton depot at the end of Main Street where passenger trains stopped coming in the 1940s. In my mind's eye, the sun is always shining, and I see him swinging down from a railway car, the flaxen hair, the trim uniform, his canvas army bag slung over his shoulder.

"Probably," I say, temporizing, feeling terrible, "How are you Daddy?"

"I'm not well at all. I'm in pretty bad shape. Can you come and get me, Pam? I'm not in good shape at all."

At ninety-six, he's not in good shape; my only comfort is that he's living in a good place.

Tending the Gibbs Graves

Out in Castleton recently, we had a day of perfect fall weather. The sun was bright, and there was a light breeze. It was in the thirties overnight, but twenty degrees warmer by noon. Best of all, the air was full of that autumn smell of crunchy old dry leaves.

I told my sister that it was time to drive over to Hillside Cemetery and clean up the plantings around the Gibbs headstone. I'd never taken a proprietary interest in maintaining the plot until 2007 when my father and mother were buried there.

Before that, it was tended by Aunt Alma. Every spring, she planted a double row of red geraniums.

When my Uncle Stan returned to Castleton, he took over from Alma, and he planted geraniums too and went up every few days to break off the dead blooms.

After Stan died, his daughter, my cousin Sandra who lives in Maine, hired Junior Paolino from Fair Haven to keep putting in these geraniums.

I never much kept track of this.

But when my father died, it was different. For one thing, by that time the Gibbs plot was nearly full. My grandparents had six children, and except for Aunt Alma, they all married people from right around here.

My mother died in 1990 and chose to be cremated, I think mainly because she'd been a beauty most of her life, but in the end, after years of illness, she wasn't. I think she was glad to get rid of her body.

My father dutifully said he guessed he'd be cremated too, but I told him, "That's not going to happen."

My mother's little box of ashes was buried in Fair Haven alongside my Hayes grandparents. My grandmother was in Fair Haven only because her West Haven family cemetery was full. Most of the Fair Haven cemetery is beautiful, but not my grandparents' flat sandy section.

I'd decided that my father wasn't going to spend eternity with his parents, to whom he'd never been close, and more importantly, I decided that my parents weren't going to be over in Fair Haven when the Gibbs relatives, with whom they'd spent all of their lives, were together in Castleton in the Gibbs family plot.

So, after he died, and after the cousins all said, Sure, it was OK, I had my father buried in Hillside Cemetery, and I had my mother's ashes brought over to Castleton and, I thought appropriately, put into my father's casket.

That's when taking care of the Gibbs plot became important to me. Instead of geraniums, I thought it would be nice to have a cottage garden-type bed of annuals.

Plus, I wanted to bring over some of my grandfather's perennials from his last home, which is now the Castleton Community Center, but none of his plants existed any more.

Finally, I just appropriated some of what came in for our Castleton Village Store flower boxes, geraniums and tall yellow chrysanthemums, ageratum and dusty miller.

It was adequate, but not spectacular, and since I hadn't done too well planting and maintaining, I was determined that this year I would manage a conscientious clean up.

My sister and I drove up North Road with our clippers and spades and a plastic, bushel-sized tub for hauling away plant debris. We turned into Brown Farm Road, always a dirt lane between corn fields planted by Farmer Eagan, but about to become a four house subdivision.

At the cemetery plot, I spoke, as I always do, to the headstones, to Aunt Bertha Hinkley Gibbs from Shrewsbury, the life of the party who in 1986 was the first to die, her husband my Uncle Gibby, then to Aunt Ruth Seward Gibbs and Uncle Stan, to my grandparents, Claude Gibbs who lived from 1877 to 1953, and his wife Sarah Fish Gibbs who lived from 1882 to 1954.

The Gibbs family, left to right, first row: Alma, Claude and Sadie, Stan, second row Harold, Constance, the author's mother Geraldine Gibbs Hayes, her twin brother Gerald. (Gibbs family collection)

My father's life-long Fair Haven friend Uncle Nelson Lyons lies on the other side of the plot with his wife my Aunt Connie, and then there are my parents.

My mother's twin brother Uncle Gerald Gibbs, with his wife Aunt Peg Paige is buried across the state in her family's East Barnard church graveyard.

The one who I always miss and feel should be here is my Aunt Alma. She chose to be buried with her husband Uncle Dick in the grand Donchian family tomb in Hartford, Connecticut.

My sister and I made short work of our clean-up. The sun shone bright and warm. A plane flew overhead, so far up it couldn't be seen. Except for insect hum, that was the only sound.

I didn't tell my sister this, but I often hear murmuring and laughter, like adults in another room, when unexpectedly I come up to my aunts' and uncles' graves. They were devoted to their parents. They were always together having a good time, and theirs was a life of family parties.

One of my greatest satisfactions is that now my mother and father are with them once again.

The Saint Mark's World

S aint Mark's Church, the little 1889 Episcopal chapel in the center of Castleton, is now abandoned and for sale. It's looking pretty battered, and it's hard to think what use could be made of it, or who a potential buyer would be. I had a lot of adventures in this place, none of which as I look back, were particularly religious.

I was brought up in the Federated Church down the street. I was baptized in the Federated Church, as was my father and my grandfather. My parents were married in that church. But when I was at Castleton State College, I had a gung-ho Episcopalian roommate from Connecticut, and she took me with her several Sunday mornings to Saint Mark's.

I'd never experienced anything like Saint Mark's. The building's interior felt like a little barn, full of the smell of dust and long-ago incense. We knelt continually, and across the tiny aisle CSC history professor Doctor Patterson and Mrs. Patterson carried on like dervishes.

They held classy little ancient leather prayer books; they leapt to their feet; they sank to their knees; they genuflected; they recited King James Bible-style affirmations.

I loved it.

When my husband and I returned to Castleton to live, that first Sunday, my husband asked, did we want to go to the Federated Church? And I surprised myself by saying, "No, let's go to Saint Mark's."

I thought it would just be for that first week, but I was wrong because Father Graham took one look at us and decided that we weren't going to get away.

The Saint Mark's community in the 1970s was right out of E. F. Benson's *Mapp and Lucia* books. It was a very high-church, closed community of a select, distinguished, often eccentric, few. Our priest was young charismatic Father Malcolm Montrose Graham.

Monty—as he was known—had grown up in a wealthy New York suburb, the son of an investment banker. He rejected with a vengeance both his background and his father's values.

He lived in the next-door rectory, full of crucifixes and framed medieval grave rubbings, with his wife Marion and their young son and daughter.

Strong winds of change were just starting to buffet the national Episcopal Church, and Monty himself was one who could always be counted on to push the envelope. But the institution seemed so rooted in comfortable tradition at the local, Vermont level that it wasn't possible to imagine what was looming.

Once we'd come to Saint Mark's that first Sunday, we never left. This little church became the center of our lives. There were a small number of town-resident-parishioners, and the Pattersons were absolutely characteristic of this group.

Some of the others were author and former Manhattan advertising executive Keith Jennison and his wife Emily, Mrs. Count Orlowski, old time radio actress Betty Johnson, (her husband Earl had been the voice of *The*

Shadow in a long-running radio mystery series) musician Chester Jones, and the Crane family who owned the 1810 Gift Shop.

All Doctor Patterson's degrees were from Yale. Even legendary CSC Dean, Miss Black, was on our books.

None of our fellow Saint Markians were from Castleton. Most of them weren't even from Vermont. They were from worldly, big-city places, and many had worldly, big-city pasts.

There was also a shadow world of local Episcopalians we never saw because they never, ever, came to church—not even on Christmas and Easter.

Eventually, my husband was made head of the stewardship committee and was sent out to all the officially-listed Episcopalians to ask them to pledge.

That's when I was astonished to learn, for example, that Gordon Rinquist, the one-time head of the college dining hall, and his large family, who lived out by the Allen brothers' farm in Hubbardton, were Episcopalians.

The Jennisons and the Cranes and Betty Johnson could be counted on to be in the squeaky little pews every Sunday and on the many other special days that Monty had decided to celebrate liturgically.

They were dependably faithful, but the relentless concern was that our numbers never grew. And we had no money. The Episcopal diocese was subsidizing us, and our official status was that of a mission station.

We could be closed at any time, and it would probably have been the financially prudent thing for the diocese to do.

The rashly idealistic Monty didn't help matters. On one annual pledge drive, Monty drove over to Fair Haven to the grand marble house of the wealthy, prominent Allens, another only-on-the-books local Episcopal family, and confronted them.

He told them he was not prepared to accept their money—they'd given generously for years—without their also being willing to come to church.

After this grand ultimatum, the startled, but polite Allen who opened the door said in essence, "Well, alright," and Monty never received another cent.

He always recounted this to us as a great moral victory.

▲▲▲

I don't know how long Father Monty Graham led Castleton's Saint Mark's Episcopal Church. He was there when we arrived, and we saw him off. Over the course of the period we knew him, he grew increasingly restless.

The people who went to Saint Mark's Church in the seventies were people whom Monty liked. The place was really an exclusive club.

We all felt bonded, and we all felt special.

I now understand cults with charismatic leaders. The world recedes in that sort of intense, inbred community.

We had a round of activities outside of Sunday services. I remember the first time the Episcopal bishop came down from Rock Point to visit. After— I want to say Mass, but somehow we didn't call it that—we all trooped over to Gladys Orlowski's grand house across the street to have tea. Gladys's husband, the Count, was Catholic so he stayed away.

In that first year after my husband and I had been pulled body and soul into the Saint Mark's community, I also remember my going once a week down to the Willem Leenman's at 47 Main Street to hear religion lectures that had just been given at Dartmouth and taped, and then driven over the mountain to Castleton and played for a little group of us devotees.

Waiting for the week's lecture to arrive, we sat around the front room listening to Weston Priory records. The Leenman brand of Protestant Christianity wasn't as ornate as ours over at Saint Mark's, but it also was intense.

Later in the seventies, we Saint Markians started having pot luck suppers in the church basement, which was predictably tiny and dark.

I remember Monty once telling me that he would give me a free hand in redecorating it. But I knew that there was almost nothing that could be done down there.

However, the basement on late fall evenings was a cozy spot. It was like being safe in a cave with all your best friends. We had candles and everyone brought wonderful food. We sat at tables which were old cable spools. That's where I first got to know local author Keith Jennison.

Upstairs in the tiny sanctuary, we followed what sometimes felt like an English liturgical calendar from the 1930s. For example, during Lent, Monty told us that Mothering Sunday was coming up, and he gave everyone a recipe for Simnel cake, which looked ingredient-wise like something that had come

St. Mark's Church. (Pamela Hayes Rehlen photo)

out of England when post World War Two rationing was still in effect.

I went home and made this Simnel cake, and it was delicious. We all brought our cakes in and shared them after church. Last time I looked, I still had the recipe.

On Palm Sunday, Monty, gloriously robed, led us three times around the church building—and that wasn't much of a trek- usually through thin wet snow, loudly singing entrance-to-Jerusalem type hymns.

Marion Graham was Monty's gentle, sheltered wife. I remember once she'd sat on a Rutland jury that convicted a thief. It tortured her that the man was going to be punished for his crime, and she came to me, as the only attorney in our little congregation, to ask if it would be alright to send this man some money she'd inherited.

As the seventies wore on, Monty became more extreme. One Sunday, we arrived to find that he'd spent the night before pulling out all the Saint Mark's pews.

We walked into an empty room with the floor gouged and stained. Monty told us that this was how the first Christians worshiped, standing together around an alter.

When I was pregnant with my first child, Monty was ecstatic. He started planning a baptism with every conceivable bell and whistle.

That's when I realized that I believed most in place and past. I told him that our children would be baptized in the Federated Church down the street because it was my family church and would still be there long after Saint Mark's was gone.

It was the only time I was ever frank with Monty. I always accommodated him, and that made me an 'extreme-ritual enabler.'

When Count Orlowski died, my husband went to the funeral at Saint John's right across the street from Saint Mark's and came home to say, after this first Catholic experience, how plain and 'low church' the funeral Mass had been.

But Monty was slowly moving away from high church Anglicism toward the mysticism of Russian Orthodoxy. He bought icons and started singing different hymns.

And then one day Monty told us that he would be leaving Saint Mark's, and entering a Russian Orthodox monastery. Their children were going off to private schools. Marion would be joining a Russian Orthodox convent not far from her husband.

An era was over. The people we knew then are now almost all gone and by a long route I've come home to Roman Catholicism.

Little St. Mark's is now abandoned and for sale.

Castleton's
Pink House

L arry Ward sold his father's place to my husband and me because he had gone to the Castleton Normal School with my mother and always thought of her as 'Queen of the Campus.'

That's how he'd inscribed his graduation picture. I think I still have it somewhere. As a little kid I remember seeing that photo of handsome Larry, written across it in big flowing script: "To Gerry Gibbs Queen of the Campus."

I always give her credit for our being able, in the mid-seventies, to buy what turned into Castleton's pink house.

Maybe, to some extent, my mother *was* 'Queen of the Campus.' She was a beauty, friendly, lively, involved in all the Normal School activities. Perhaps, Larry had a little crush on her, although he was a life-long bachelor and not very interested in women.

Larry's mother was a Langdon. The Langdons are Castleton's oldest family, and over the years they came to own several of the town's oldest and finest houses. Larry's aunts shared an ancient residence immediately to the west of the Federated Church, and Larry's parents had the 1818 Georgian style, Thomas Dake designed house on the corner of Castleton's Mill and Main Streets.

The Wards were not happy in their marriage. Being practical old-time Vermonters, instead of divorcing, they divided their house in half, ran a cardboard partition up the front staircase, and lived separate lives. Larry, an only child, wound up with his father John in the east side of the house.

After he graduated from the Normal School, Larry was probably too shy and retiring to be an effective teacher, but he was a gifted amateur botanist. He went to work as a gardener for a UVM professor. He rode the bus back and forth to Burlington, and in later years came home only on week-ends to look after his father.

By then, old John Ward suffered from dementia and lived alone in the ell. Mrs. Ward must have died. In the best of times, it had been a precarious *Ethan Frome* sort of household.

CSC professor Bob Patterson told me that he and his wife Marilyn, who lived close by on Mill Street, would go over and try to help their elderly irrational neighbor. But there wasn't much they could do.

After John Ward died, Larry stayed in Burlington full time, and the house sat abandoned. My husband and I would walk by and peek in the windows. We saw that the rooms were filled floor to ceiling with old magazines. Out in back around the ell, masses of hybrid day lilies that Larry had cross pollinated bloomed under the trees.

Larry wasn't coming back to Castleton and couldn't afford, on his gardener's salary, to pay the taxes and maintain this old deteriorating building. He probably didn't know what to do.

My husband, very young at the time but always eager to rescue old places, started to ask around. I think he finally called Larry in Burlington, and he must have called at just the right moment.

Others in town had also approached Larry, but if young John Rehlen's wife was the daughter of Geraldine Gibbs, Larry said that he'd sell his house to us. This is what he did, and he then returned to his Burlington gardens and his day lily hybridizations with a great weight off his shoulders.

We soon found that Larry Ward's beautiful old house was grander on the outside than in. This is an early 19th century building probably built by the local master house joiner Thomas Dake.

It has many of his signature touches. The exterior swags and rosettes on the frieze and the gable end embellishment point to a period in town history when there was money here and a high degree of architectural sophistication.

Before the railroad came to Rutland, Castleton seemed destined to be a commercial center and many of the houses along Main Street are richly deco-rated and architecturally grand.

But over the years, the beautiful Ward house had been put to other uses and the inside had been stripped bare. Some previous owner had taken out the original six fireplaces. All the interior decorative moldings were gone. The early flat staircase had been ripped out and replaced with a wide straight shot staircase (then divided by the Wards' cardboard partition.)

We were told that in the 1930s this building was a hardware store and a funeral parlor. Out in the ell, we found an overhead pulley and a loading dock for caskets.

On top of all of this, when we bought the building, we could hardly get through the rooms. Old John Ward was a hoarder. He held on to everything, and for years had lived only in his primitive kitchen with a slate sink, a hand pump, and a rocking chair pulled up close to a big cast iron range.

▲▲▲

After Larry Ward sold us his family place, we realized we had a near-wreck on our hands. Still, my young husband was jubilant. This was going to be a chal-lenge worthy of the talents he suspected he possessed. There was nothing he enjoyed more than the idea of saving and restoring an old house. It was like bringing a dying elderly relative back to vigorous health and long life.

Everything about the Ward House was graceful. It was exquisitely designed. It faced south, and sunlight filled all the front rooms. Around the ell, little trees had over the years grown up creating a leafy glade, and there were great banks of Larry's day lilies.

Sounds of college commotion seldom reached this end of town. The place exemplified the atmosphere of old Castleton. It was like the story book princess who had fallen asleep and dreamed away for a hundred years as the world changed around her.

Three people had principle roles helping my husband restore the Ward House. There was Bryan Kelly. He was the one to first head into that vast, dirty, jumbled, repository of saved-everything.

Bryan was physically strong and temperamentally cheerful. He loved this kind of work. For awhile, he had been doing debris clean-up jobs for us around the store and at my grandmother's house in Fair Haven. He took on clearing out the Ward house with gusto, and he worked there for months.

What I remember most were the ceiling-high piles of *Life* magazines. These had to be hauled to the dump. Predictably, there were also mountains of Larry's seed catalogues. Every bit of mail that had ever come into that house was still there. For forty years, nothing had been thrown away.

One day Bryan got to the point where he could tear down the house's cardboard partitions. Light came flooding into the dirty old rooms. Against the walls, gradually revealed as the clean-out continued, particularly back where John Ward had lived, we found primitive 19th and even 18th century cupboard pieces, probably from the first-town-settler Langdons, John Ward's wife's family.

We also came across woven reed baskets with distinctive lacy collars. I saved these, although most of then were in pretty rough shape.

I'm glad I did because years later I read in the *Vermont Historical Society Magazine* about the few remaining native Indian tribes living in Vermont in the 1920s and 30s.

These tribe members often supported themselves by weaving reed baskets which they sold door to door to Vermont farm wives. Their baskets all had decorative collars, and these were the baskets that old John Ward had scattered in with his mountains of magazines.

It was a bleak and dismal sight when Bryan finally finished more or less emptying the house. During the place's hardware store years, with a savage thoroughness, every architectural embellishment had been removed.

All the fireplaces were gone, and my husband calculated that there had originally been six. This house was built at a time when houses were still being heated with fireplaces and not with the parlor stoves that soon after took their place.

Once again, my mother came to the rescue. After being Larry Ward's 'Queen of the Campus' at the Normal, her first job as pretty, stylish elemen-

Castleton's Pink House. (Pamela Hayes Rehlen photo)

tary school teacher Miss Gibbs was in Middletown Springs. One of her pupils was little Thereon 'Buddy' Krause.

My husband wanted to put all six fireplaces back, but it was nearly impossible to find a mason willing and able to do that kind of extensive historic restoration.

As my mother's student, Bud Krause's interests had been more vocational than academic, and my mother was concerned about this. But she shouldn't have worried because Bud grew up to be an outstanding craftsman, specifically a master mason.

He had all the work he wanted, and he would never have taken on my husband's Ward House project except that, like Larry, he came to realize that John Rehlen's wife was Miss Gibbs's daughter. He remembered his teacher fondly, and he said for that reason he'd fit rebuilding the fireplaces into his already full schedule.

For my husband, it wasn't just the architectural details that had to be worked on. The house had to be insulated, and it needed new plumbing and wiring as well as a furnace. The days of heating with a coal range in the back kitchen were over.

Also, we were going to have to have someone do a lot of restorative carpentry. We'd had Castletonian Dick Gray do work for us at the Manse. He'd built bookshelves for me. Now, we had to see if he was willing to take on a pretty daunting job.

▲▲▲

Once Bud Krause had finished rebuilding the Ward House's chimneys and six fireplaces, my husband wanted to restore the building's interior. He also wanted to rebuild the front staircase which had been ripped out in the 1930s.

Dick Gray, our carpenter, was a nearly life-long Castleton boy. He lived at the end of South Street where the road turns east and uphill toward Pond Hill

Stables. He's dead now, and I can't ask him, but he probably knew the Ward House in its hardware store days.

My husband showed Dick the black and white photos of interiors he'd found in Herbert Wheaton Congdon's *Old Houses of Vermont*. For a bio-chem. major, my husband had turned out to be surprisingly good at researching historic architecture.

Whatever he thought of our plan—probably that it was going to be time consuming and expensive—Dick settled down to his assignment, and today the Pink House west sitting room fireplace is an exact copy of the Farrar-Mansur House bedroom mantel in Weston.

It was hard to know how to proceed with the hall stairway. Looking back, those were exciting days. We were young and full of energy, and there was a little group of us with a common purpose. We were often in strategy-huddles with my sister, Bryan Kelly, Dick Gray and any Castleton old-timer passers-by who wanted to add their two cents.

When the 1930's stairway came down, we found faint scribing on plank walls indicating how the original staircase had been, and there were old fascia boards which gave us a pattern to follow.

The original staircase had been an early box style running from west to east. It would never have worked for a store. It would have been impossible to get anything cumbersome up stairs like these.

As Dick finished his restorative carpentry, it came time to repaint. The exterior of the house had been minimally maintained, but it was still white. I think we expected to repaint it white, but then one day my husband and I visited Manchester.

South of town on the east side of Route 30, we drove past a very old house shaded by giant maples with a deep bed of hostas and a lush front lawn.

This may or may not have been the one-time home of Vermont regionalist author Dorothy Canfield Fisher. (Fisher had also lived in Arlington.) However, for me the most significant thing about it was that it was painted pink.

I loved it, and I decided that we were going to paint the Ward House the same pink. I didn't realize then that it's almost impossible to exactly duplicate paint colors. This is the reason that, over the years, our pink house color has sometimes been more, sometimes less, pleasing.

One decade's harsh cotton candy shade—nothing like the paint chip from which it was taken—verged on disaster, but I've never changed my mind about the color pink.

For years, tourists traveling through town would stop at our Castleton Village Store, often when I was working, to complain about the color of the house down at the end of Main Street.

I would shake my head in sympathy with their outrage and not let on that I was the culprit. But I think over the years the pink house has come to look less shockingly unusual. No one has complained in a long time. Maybe there are more old pink houses now in Vermont, or at least in New England.

I failed to realize when we first painted the Ward House that the Manchester prototype was surrounded with masses of light-softening vegetation. In contrast, our pink house was on a bright, barren corner lot. This made the unusual color all the more jarring.

However, our spot has grown up—although never so lushly as in Manchester Village—and a while ago we planted two oaks in front of the house, which helps.

Over the decades since we bought and restored it, we've rented the Pink House to a number of people. Our most illustrious tenants were Keith and Emily Jennison. When Keith moved in, he looked around, pleased with everything, and said, "This is it. The only way I'll leave here is feet first."

The Pink House and the Jennisons were a perfect match. The couple filled the place with books and antiques, framed autographed photographs of famous writers, old oriental rugs, and two cats.

Keith was a well known author and retired editor, the originator of large print books. He taught a writing course at CSC. *Rutland Herald* people came out to talk with him about journalistic practices.

During the many years the Jennisons lived there, the Pink House became a pilgrimage destination. A steady stream of the couple's many admirers drove out from Rutland to visit.

Emily wasn't able to, but Keith finished his life in this house.

About the Author

Pamela Hayes Rehlen attended Castleton State College and graduated from Middlebury College and Boston University Law School. This is her second book. She's written all of her life.

Acknowledgements

This book would never have been written if it weren't for a number of fortunate occurrences and the contributions of many people. First of all, I owe so much to *Rutland Herald* Managing Editor Randal Smathers who got things going, and then, several years later, was willing to go over all of my columns and several *Rutland Herald* People and Places articles and select for me the pieces that he thought should be included in a book collection.

Right after him, I want to recognize retired *Newsday* editor, and my longtime friend, Tony Marro who is always to me — and to many people — wonderfully supportive and encouraging.

I have to thank my son for once again providing me with a book cover photograph, my sister Holly Hitchcock for generously hunting around and finding old family pictures, Rob Staudter, down at our store office, for patiently defeating technical challenges, and my husband for being a good listener.

The book designers Ron Toelke and Barbara Kempler-Toelke were accomplished, accommodating, and always terrifically easy to work with.

I also have to recognize the contributions of the many, many Castleton people I interviewed over a three year period. I still marvel that when I called and asked for an interview no one ever turned me down. Everyone was generous and forthcoming. They told me unforgettable stories.

Of course, finally, there's my father Rex Hayes. I wish he were still here so I could thank him for conveying to me his love of the place from which he came, his delight in other people, and his unique point of view.

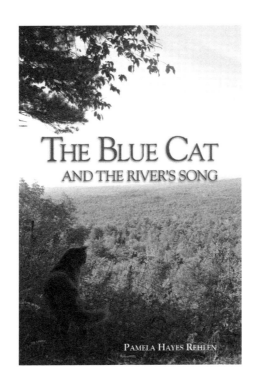

Also By Pamela Hayes Rehlen

The Blue Cat and the River's Song can be ordered from:

The Castleton Village Store

P. O. Box 275

Castleton, Vermont 05735